◆ Underground   P Parking

HUDSON RIVER

EAST RIVER

EAST RIVER

UPPER BAY

Map 1

Map 2

Map 3

Map 4

Map 5

N

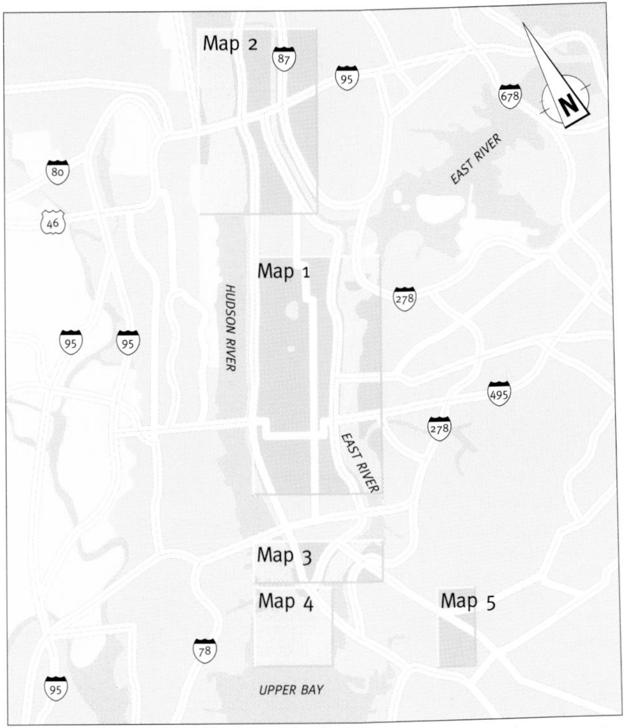

First United States Edition

ISBN 0-8212-2156-6

Library of Congress Catalog Card Number
94-78808

Bulfinch Press is an imprint and trademark
of Little, Brown and Company (Inc.)
Published simultaneously in Canada by
Little, Brown & Company (Canada) Limited

PRINTED IN SINGAPORE

ART IN *focus*

NEW YORK

Anna Gendel

A Bulfinch Press Book
Little, Brown and Company
Boston • New York • Toronto • London

CONTENTS

New York presents the visitor with a vast array of artistic and architectural treasures, and the choice of places to visit can seem overwhelming. This book is intended to provide a guide to the city's top attractions, so that the tourist with limited time to spend can make an informed choice about what to see. Although it contains what most would agree to be the city's artistic highlights, the selection is personal; the aim has been to present the best rather than the most comprehensive collection of venues and works of art. The wealth and energy of New York is reflected in its wide range of architectural styles and artistic holdings, most of which are not native to the city. Indeed, the art of native New York State plays a small part in the collections of the city, especially since the larger part of the collection of the Museum of the American Indian relocated to Washington DC.

The European discoverer of the island of Manhattan in 1524 was the Italian navigator Giovanni da Verazzano. Dutch traders inhabited the island between 1613 and 1667, but evidence of their activities is sparse. No seventeenth-century architecture has survived, and traces of Dutch rule are limited to the odd geographic reference and material such as the restrained but authoritative eighteenth-century portrait of Peter Stuyvesant (1), the last Dutch governor of the city between 1647 and 1664. The Dutch called their settlement New Amsterdam, but when it was captured by the British in 1664 it was renamed New York, after the Duke of York, later James II.

From the British occupation of New York there remain two important examples of colonial architecture, one religious, the other secular. Obscured

1. HENRI COUTURIER
(ATTRIBUTED)
*PORTRAIT OF PETER
STUYVESANT,*
EIGHTEENTH CENTURY,
(NEW-YORK
HISTORICAL SOCIETY)

2. John James Audubon, *A Wild Turkey*, 1820 (New York Historical Society)

by the skyscrapers of Wall Street is St. Paul's church (1766), a crude derivation of Saint Martin-in-the-Fields in London, built while the population of the city numbered 25,000 and the site was a wheat field. At the other end of the island, in an equally rural setting, Colonel and Mrs. Morris built their suburban villa in 1768, now the Morris-Jumel Mansion (page 93). During the War of Independence Colonel Morris returned to England and his wife and children left the city. In 1776 the house was taken over by George Washington, who from this high point was able to command strategic views down the length of the island, and to both rivers.

It was not be until the early twentieth century that this part of northern Manhattan was built over. On his return from England where he had made a small fortune from the subscription and publication of his *Birds of America* (2), John James Audubon bought an estate of thirty acres at neighbouring Washington Heights. A romantic figure, Audubon had travelled throughout the United States to record 1,065 species of birds which were illustrated in the 435 plates of a lavish 'double elephant folio' edition, published between 1827 and 1838.

The period starting with Independence in 1776 and stretching past the Civil War and into the late nineteenth century saw New York grow as state capital (it was also briefly national capital, 1789–90). Ironically, independence and phenomenal prosperity did not really bring a new cultural identity. Derivations of European prototypes predominated in most forms of art, and by the later part of the nineteenth century New York private collections were very rich in examples of European art of the highest quality. This was the generation of the super-rich tycoons, the fledgling 'squillionaires', whose wealth was boosted by the lack of any form of income tax between 1880 and 1913 .

Magnates such as J. Pierpont Morgan, Henry and Louise Havermayer, Henry Clay Frick, Andrew Carnegie, the Whitneys, the Warburgs, the Astors, and John D. Rockefeller Jr. left collections, bequests and foundations that bear testimony to their personal interests and concerns, but the civic patronage of New York also worked, and continued to flourish,

3. (LEFT) AN ANONYMOUS QUILT (AMERICAN MUSEUM OF FOLK ART). 4. (RIGHT) EDWARD HICKS, *THE PEACEABLE KINGDOM*, C. 1840–45 (BROOKLYN MUSEUM)

on an important corporate level. Both the Metropolitan Museum of Art and later the Museum of Modern Art were established by committees of the rich and influential, and have continued to prosper from their bequests, and the involvement of their successors. Indeed, it is only with an awareness of these benefactions that a clear understanding of the city's heritage can be formed. Many donors gave to museums on the understanding that their collections remain intact. So a visitor to the Metropolitan Museum who wants to see its finest Early Italian Renaissance art will find important works in the main collection, chronologically arranged, but also in the Robert Lehmann Wing and in the Jack and Belle Linsky Wing.

The great industrial fortunes not only formed fantastic, lavish collections, they also shaped the appearance and disposition of the city. At the turn of the twentieth century New York was formed by two strains of building; the block-long mansions built in predominantly historic styles; Neo-Renaissance for J. P. Morgan, Louis XVIII for Frick, and vaguely Neo-Renaissance for Carnegie. While industries and corporations were increasingly looking to modern engineering for corporate architecture and the vertical proclamations of power inherent in skyscraper design, domestic architecture remained resolutely retrospective. Frank Lloyd Wright's modern domestic architecture and interior design, for example, is represented in New York only by the Little Room of 1912–14 which was transported over a considerable distance from Minnesota (page 90).

That most spectacular American impulse – to transport and reinstall parts of historic buildings and whole rooms – was done either as a grandiose form of collecting, or as a lavish didactic display. In 1899 the great financier J. Pierpont Morgan bought the eleven panels of Fragonard's *Progress of Love* for $310,000 and installed them at his London house in Prince's Gate. On Morgan's death in 1913 the art dealer Joseph Duveen bought them and soon managed to sell them on, at a healthy profit, to Henry Clay Frick (page 43). Also in 1913, the American sculptor George Grey Barnard was about to inaugurate the museum of medieval architectural fragments and sculpture he had assembled on Fort Washington Avenue. This was the first incarnation of The Cloisters, a collection that might have been dispersed when Barnard ran out of money in the 1920s had it not been for John D. Rockefeller, Jr.. Rockefeller not only bought most of the collection, but paid for its relocation to its current site (page 32).

Henry Clay Frick – An Avid Collector

The Frick Collection is one of the gems of New York; indeed it is generally regarded as one of the finest small museums in the world, displaying a collection of outstandingly high quality in a delightful setting. Its founder was Henry Clay Frick (1849–1919), an industrialist from Pennsylvania who made a fortune in coke and steel. There was nothing artistic in his background, but he loved paintings from an early age. When he applied for a loan at the age of twenty-one, the bank reported: 'On job all day, keeps books evenings, may be a little too enthusiastic about pictures, but not anough to hurt...advise making loan.' By the time he was thirty he was a millionaire.

Initially Frick's purchases were somewhat provincial, including paintings by artists local to Pittsburgh (the city where he made his fortune). He only began buying foreign art during the 'Grand Tour' of Europe he undertook with Andrew Mellon, future founder of the National Gallery of Washington, in 1880. Even then the paintings he bought were contemporary and academic. It was not until after the turn of century that he began to buy works of the calibre seen in his collection today.

In 1905 he moved to New York, and in 1913–14 built the splendid mansion that is now the Frick Collection. With the construction of the house and the assimilation of works such as Fragonard's *Progress of Love* (5) from J. Pierpont Morgan's estate, Frick had taken on his New York peers. From the first he intended his home to become a museum and he conceived it as a monument to his taste. The mansion

5. JEAN-HONORÉ FRAGONARD, *THE LOVER CROWNED* FROM *THE PROGRESS OF LOVE* SERIES, 1771–3, (FRICK COLLECTION)

was built specifically to protect and enhance the collection, and the furniture and decorative parts it displays are of as high a quality as the paintings. Frick always considered whether a prospective purchase would fit the character of the house, and the pictures tend to be intimate in character, as befits a private residence (although there are some grand showpieces). They are not displayed in any chronological or geographical sequence, but where they complement one other, and one of the pleasures of visiting the collection is the impression of randomly 'finding' masterpieces. The collection opened to the public in 1935, and Frick left a large fund to maintain it. Occasionally the trustees purchase works of art, but only when the work will match the quality and character of the collection. The Frick remains the most complete and unified example of private collecting on a grand scale that is accessible to the public in New York.

6. (LEFT) GEORGES DE LA TOUR *THE PENITENT MAGDALENE*, *C.* 1638–43 (METROPOLITAN MUSEUM OF ART). 7. (RIGHT) JOHN SINGER SARGENT *MME X.*, 1884 (METROPOLITAN MUSEUM OF ART).

The authority of European culture was such that collectors with avant-garde tastes, such as Mr. and Mrs. Henry O. Havermeyer, bought all the most modern painters, from Monet to Cézanne. But when their elder daughter Electra reacted to her parents' taste by collecting Americana her mother was outraged: 'How can you, Electra, you, who have been brought up with Rembrandts and Manets live with such American trash?'

At the turn of the century, the circulation of big money in New York established an interesting cycle of patronage. Tycoons with vast industrial fortunes who were living in revivalist mansions and collecting old masters were simultaneously erecting skyscrapers for their corporations or – like Rockefeller and his 'city within a city' at Rockefeller Center – for investment. The new profile of the city, a dramatic spectacle of unparalleled modernity, at the skyline and on the streets, was a rich source of imagery for modern American artists – the art of the city concerned with itself.

'The Eight' later known as 'The Ash Can School' became a group, informally led by Robert Henri, after their rejection from the Academy of Design in 1907. Although there was no common stylistic programme amongst the painters apart from their rebellion against academic idealism, they banded together for an alternative exhibition space at the Macbeth Galleries of New York, and gradually grew to be associated with a shared interest in urban subject matter. William J. Glackens' *Hammerstein's Roof Garden* of about 1901 (9) is to some extent indebted to the work of French artists such as Manet, Toulouse-Lautrec, or Seurat in that its subject is the urban phenomenon of popular and highly fashionable entertainment. Despite the fascination of the city for young American painters such as The Eight, scenes such as Glackens' remain rooted in an Edwardian style that was highly dependent on Impressionism.

This situation was fundamentally disrupted in 1913 by the Armory Show, one of the most influential exhibitions ever held. Its official title was the International Exhibition of Modern Art, but its popular name comes from that it was held at the 69th Regiment Armory. It consisted of 13,000 works by 'progressive and live artists' ranging from Goya and Ingres to Matisse. For many American artists it was their first serious encounter with modern painting and sculpture and for several of them it decisively changed the direction of their careers. There also emerged a new generation of collectors and patrons sympathetic to modern ideas in art. One of the most important of these was Mrs. Gertrude Vanderbilt Whitney, granddaughter of Cornelius 'Commodore' Vanderbilt who conceived Grand Central Station (page 51). Although her own work as a sculptress was traditional, she supported many young artists who worked in experimental styles, providing them with congenial places to meet and show their work. In 1929 she offered her superb collection of modern American art to the Metropolitan Museum and when her gift was refused she founded her own museum two years later – the Whitney Museum of American Art.

The artist who is most widely represented at the Whitney (page 119) is Edward Hopper, whose widow bequeathed a very large collection of his work. Hopper is the most renowned exponent of American Scene Painting, a dominant strain in American art in the 1920s and 1930s. The artists who are embraced by this term were not an organized group, but they had in common the fact that they turned away from abstraction and experimental art and depicted aspects of American life and landscape in a sober naturalistic style. Hopper painted the spiritual emptiness of big city life with poignancy, conjuring a sad poetry from subjects such as gas stations at night and lonely diners.

A very different pattern of collecting was established by John D. Rockefeller Jr. The wealth of the man was so great that his father had been warned by a family friend, Frederick D. Gates, that unless some of the massive fortune was spent it would crush him, his children, and his children's children. Although John D. Rockefeller Jr. did spend and endow lavishly, his naturally sober temperament inclined him towards collecting examples of restrained, antique but excellent craftsmanship. In contrast, his wife,

8. ROCKEFELLER CENTER

9. WILLIAM GLACKENS *HAMMERSTEIN'S ROOF GARDEN*, C. 1901 (WHITNEY MUSEUM OF ART)

10. Henri Matisse *The Red Studio*, 1911 (Museum of Modern Art)

11. Maurice Prendergast *Central Park* (Whitney Museum of Art)

Abby Aldrich Rockefeller was impassioned by modern art, and her acquisitions were tolerated with good will by her husband who once remarked, 'We never lack material for lively arguments, modern art and the King James Version can forever keep us young.' In 1927 Mrs. Rockefeller started ed collecting modern art and by 1929 she had joined forces with Miss Lillie Bliss and Mrs. Cornelius J. Sullivan to establish the Museum of Modern Art (page 97). When Miss Bliss died in 1931 and left a staggering collection including twenty paintings by Cézanne; Mrs. Rockefeller raised $600,000 needed to maintain it. Furthermore, it was to a Rockefeller house that the museum moved in 1932, the present location of MoMA, which was revamped by a vast programme of expansion and renovation during the 1980s.

The establishment of collections such as those of The Museum of Modern Art in 1929, the Whitney Museum of American Art in 1931, and The Museum of Non-Objective Art (later the Guggenheim) in 1939 did not simply enrich the city; in addition they continued the effect of the Armory Show by making European modernism part of the cultural framework of New York. In addition to these large and rapidly expanding institutions, smaller commercial galleries were opened during the 1930s and 40s. One of these was Art of this Century launched in 1942 by Peggy Guggenheim, the niece of Solomon Guggenheim (the industrialist who founded the Guggenheim Museum). Peggy Guggenheim had already

Although the skyscraper was actually invented in Chicago, it is in New York that they are seen in their most dramatic context. The concentrated area of Manhattan island makes this form of vertical construction a necessity, and the street grid orders the jostling towers into spectacular perspectival vistas. The ubiquitous nature of the New York skyline, a staple image of film, photography and advertising, cannot prepare the visitor for the endless variety of striking views provided by the city, each angle providing a new and momentary composition. From the river the skyscrapers form a phalanx of facades, each displaying a different solution to the articulation of the curtain wall. On clear, luminous days the summits of the buildings are seen to their best advantage, with light glinting off the Chrysler motor-motifs, or gleaming on the golden pyramid that caps Cass Gilbert's United States Courthouse (1933).

Since the Twin Towers of the World Trade Center were inaugurated in 1976, they have remained unsurpassed as civic icons of corporate America, as much for their height as for the fact that they are exact doubles, of a form that could easily replicate itself.

Notwithstanding the way that Manhattan offers a dynamic potted history of the skyscraper, the striking effect of the buildings depends as much on juxtaposition as anything else. Every period and style of skyscraper construction can be traced the length and breadth of the island, but the erratic fortunes of New York, its booms and busts, have scattered towers across the town, with occasionally ironic effect. Hence the proximity of the Chrysler Building (page 28) – built on the American Dream of a motorcar industry that appeared invincible – to the Four Seasons Hotel (page 42) the ultimate service industry palace. Architects such as I.M.Pei, the designer of the Four Seasons, have capitalized on the possible meanings of such comparisons. His hotel is intended to match, and perhaps surpass the luxury of the age of Chrysler. The style and scale adopted by Pei is based on the modernist grandeur of the 1930s, and our vision of it as it appears in the Hollywood extravaganzas of the time.

INTRODUCTION

12. THE MANHATTAN SKYLINE AT NIGHT

13. (Left)
Willem de
Kooning
*Pirate
(Untitled 11)*,
1981 (MoMA).
14. (Right)
Andy Warhol
*Campbell's
Soup*, 1965
(MoMA)

masterminded a gallery of avant-garde art in London between 1938 and 1940 and she was on terms of close friendship with some of the most illustrious figures in the art world of her time (she was briefly married to the great German painter Max Ernst). The seminal importance of Art of this Century was that it fostered the interrelationship between European Surrealism and the Abstract Expressionism of the New York School. Guggenheim had helped and encouraged European artists and intellectuals including André Breton, Ernst, André Masson and Yves Tanguy to take refuge in New York during the war. At Art of this Century she promoted a younger generation of American artists already greatly influenced by the Surrealists; Jackson Pollock, Ad Reinhardt, Clyfford Still and Mark Rothko were all given one man shows at the gallery. Of similar

THE FEDERAL ART PROJECT

The Works Project Administration, of which the Federal Art Project was a part, was established by President Franklin D. Roosevelt in May 1935 as a way of combatting unemployment during the Depression. Direct payment of relief was replaced by work programmes designed to 'help men keep their chins up and their hands in'. Four policies were outlined as direction for the Federal Art Project; to employ artists, to educate art students, to expand art projects into rural areas, and to fund research into American cultural heritage. During the eight years it existed (1935–48) the Federal Art Project gave work to large numbers of artists. At its peak it employed over 5,000; virtually all major American artists of the period were involved at one time or another,

either as teachers or practitioners. Stuart Davis produced a mural for houses in the Williamsburg section of Brooklyn entitled *Swing Landscape*; Jackson Pollock executed about fifty paintings under the scheme and Arshile Gorky submitted a Cubist mural for one of the administrative buildings at Newark Airport. Work commissioned by the W.P.A. could take one of several forms; easel paintings; graphic images such as prints, lithographs, and woodcuts; The Index of American Design, (a collection of 22,000 watercolours recording American craft and folk art); murals; photographs; posters; sculptures; and monuments. The collections of the New York museums include many of these works, but only a few of the murals

importance was Atelier 17, an engraving studio run by the English print-maker William Stanley Hayter. Hayter had originally set up the studio in Paris, but he moved to New York in 1940, and in the almost twenty years of its existence there it provided another meeting place for emigré and native artists to explore graphic innovations based on a Surrealist approach. Hayter probably played a larger role than anyone else in the twentieth-century revival of the print as an independent art form.

Abstract Expressionism was without doubt the USA's most momentous contribution to twentieth-century art; for the first time America led and Europe followed. There was an extraordinary excitement in the art world in New York, as the city took over from Paris the position it had long held as the world capital of contemporary art. Not all the painters covered by the term Abstract Expressionism were abstract artists and not all of them were expressionist in style. However, they had in common a renunciation of traditional values and a demand for spontaneous freedom of expression. In many respects the audacity of Surrealism infected the New York School with a New World heroism which was later enhanced by the development of Action painting, a term coined by the critic Harold Rosenberg. Made manifest by the automatist doodles of Arshile Gorky, the hypnotic choreography of Jackson Pollock's drip paintings, and the fleshy sweeping strokes of Willem de Kooning, Action Painting restored Romanticism to art by means of immediate gesture and honesty of expression. De Kooning continued painting into the 1980s, but by then the heyday of Abstract Expressionism was long past. It stimulated other types of abstraction, but many artists grew away from its emotionalism and sought a cooler,

painted for public buildings survive. The most accessible of these are Edward Laning's four arched panels and two overdoors of *The Story of the Recorded Word* (1938) which can be found on the vault of the third floor lobby of the New York Public Library (15). In addition to the Federal Art Project there were a Federal Writers' Project, a Federal Theatre Project and a Federal Music Project; collectively these four are known as the Federal Arts Projects. One of the products of the Federal Writers' Project was a 1939 guidebook to the city. This was reprinted in 1982 and can still be bought today.

15. EDWARD LANING, DETAIL FROM *THE STORY OF THE RECORDED WORD*, 1938 (NEW YORK PUBLIC LIBRARY)

more restrained, less intensely serious form of expression. Minimal Art grew out of this background as did Pop Art. Pop's arch-exponent was Andy Warhol, who sprang to fame in 1962 with his pictures of Campbell's soup cans. It was Warhol's Factory, a vast warehouse/studio in which he directed and promoted art, film, and music, that most shaped New York as the arena for bohemian life in the late 1960s and 70s. The activities of Warhol's circle at The Factory were multidisciplinary, including film-making, patronage of a band called the Velvet Underground, and the production of a celebrity magazine called *Interview*. Warhol (and his assistants) produced an enormous amount of work, often using techniques such as silkscreen that allowed limitless duplication. However, Warhol also marks the beginning of a tendency for the artist's lifestyle to take over from his actual creations as the centre of interest. In much of the avant-garde art of the 1960s and after, the traditional idea of a finished 'product' has been abandoned. Performance Art and Happenings are akin to theatre in that they exist at a certain time rather than in permanent physical form and in Conceptual Art the idea behind the work is regarded as just as important as its realization. Joseph Beuys, for example, transformed his arrival in New York into an artwork in itself. *I Love America and America Loves Me* traced Beuys as he was literally unloaded from the aircraft into an ambulance, wrapped in felt which he considered to have healing and restorative properties. The ambulance then transported him to his gallery where he was locked in a cage with a coyote, symbol of native America.

New York still boasts a rich culture of commercial exhibition spaces and experimental institutions such as the Dia Center for the Arts. The avant-garde, or what was avant-garde in the past, is still located Downtown, around SoHo, whereas the more establishment galleries are scattered along 57th Street and up Madison Avenue towards the Whitney Museum. A full picture of the city's artistic life must involve these commercial venues as well as the great galleries and museums.

16. Joseph Beuys *7,000 Oaks* (Dia Center for the Arts)

ART

IN

FOCUS

Museums

Paintings

Applied Arts

Architecture

Address
40 W 53rd St.
New York,
N.Y.10019
℡ 956 3535

Map reference

How to get there
Subway: E and F.
Bus: M1, M2, M3, M4 and
M5.

Opening times
Wed to Sun, 10–5. Tue 10–8.
Closed Mon.

Entrance fee
$4.50 adults, $2 senior
citizens, free for children
under 12. Free to all on Tue
5–8.

This museum, which is dedicated to the handicrafts of the twentieth century, was established largely thanks to the efforts of Aileen Osborne Webb and the American Craft Council that she founded in 1943. A rich socialite, Webb was also a proficient watercolourist, potter, enamelist and woodcarver, who organized a cooperative for the craftsmen of Putnam County during the Depression. By 1939 the cooperative had grown into the Handicraft League of Craftsmen and three years later it merged with a fellow organization, the American Handcraft Council, to become the American Craftsmen's Cooperative Council.

The museum was first located at 29 West Fifty-third Street, a house bought by Mrs. Webb for what was then known as the Museum of Contemporary Craft. Further expansion followed and the museum moved to number 44 of the same street, when it became the American Craft Museum. The present museum is now located in part of a tower designed by the architectural firm of Kevin Roche John Dinkeloo and Associates which was inaugurated in October 1986. These expanded premises enable it to show several exhibitions of differing sizes at the same time.

The permanent collection consists of a wide range of objects crafted in diverse media including wood, ceramics, fibre, paper, metal and glass, in a gamut of styles from the most modern to the traditional. As a way of providing a context for craft and its many wide-ranging issues, the museum also collects and exhibits in related areas such as architecture, fashion, painting and sculpture. The scope of the collection is restricted to twentieth-century examples. A preoccupation with a continuing, contemporary culture of craftsmanship underlies many of the exhibitions organized at the American Craft Museum, as well as emphasizing the multicultural relevance of craft in a post-industrial society.

Built 1979

This combination of a sleek, soaring skyscraper with a top pediment – the type of flourish more often associated with craftsmanship, and specifically that of the eighteenth-century furniture designer, Thomas Chippendale – has marked the design of the American Telephone and Telegraph Building with a typical Post-Modern contradiction, or eclecticism. This was the first of the corporate towers to abandon the sober dictum of the International Style: 'Form follows function'. The Chippendale quotation of the top underlines the fact that architecture can borrow from different sources as freely and irreverently as any other art form.

When the design was first aired by the team of architects led by Philip Johnson and John Burgee in 1979, the project raised some criticism for its witty, knowing design. However, the grandeur of its public spaces, accessible through a Neo-Renaissance arcade, and the finish of the Stony Creek rose-grey granite have earned the building widespread recognition.

Address
550 Madison Avenue, between 55 & 56th Streets, on the east side. New York

Map reference

How to get there
Subway: 4, 5, 6, F, E, R
Bus: M1, M2, M3, M4, M32, M28, M30.

Opening times
9–5 daily.

Entrance fee
Free.

BROOKLYN BRIDGE

Built 1879

Address
Brooklyn Bridge, City Hall Park, New York

Map reference

How to get there
Subway: 4, 5, 6, J, M, Z, 2, 3
Bus: M15, M22, M9.

Opening times
Always open.

Entrance fee
Free.

The world's first steel suspension bridge was designed in 1879 by John A. Roebling, a Prussian immigrant who developed a form of wire rope for use on canal barges that was strong enough for large structures such as bridges. However, it was not just the cables which ensured the technological success of Brooklyn Bridge. Like the skyscraper, a contemporary engineering phenomenon, the bridge was as visually impressive as it was functional. The roadway – trussed with iron girders to support it – ran suspended across the East River to provide the first universally accessible link to Brooklyn.

The sense of weightless suspension is enhanced by the inclined stays which provide extra stability, and by the contrast with the dark stone towers through which the roadway runs. Amongst New York artists the reaction was quite positive the bridge influenced paintings by Georgia O'Keeffe and John Marin, and the celebrated photograph by Margaret Burke White.

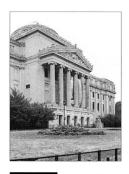

The roots of the Brooklyn Museum can be traced back to 1823 when the Brooklyn Apprentices' Library Association was founded with its core collection. Between 1896 and 1897 the present building by McKim, Mead and White was built as the West Wing of the Central Museum of The Brooklyn Institute of Arts and Sciences. A good measure of the impetus behind the establishment and building of the museum was a conviction that the commercial expansion of Manhattan would force the wealthy of that island to move to Brooklyn. What had not been reckoned with was the advent of the skyscraper, which enabled Manhattan to accommodate both its commercial and residential boom by growing upwards rather than outwards.

The Brooklyn Museum was recently renovated by the architectural firms of Arata Isozaki & Associates and James Stewart Polshek and Partners. The revamping was intended to complement as faithfully as possible the original Beaux-Arts design. The Ethnographic collection includes displays of the cultures of Oceania and the Americas, and African art. The museum is particularly rich in its collection of Egyptian art which can be seen exhibited in new galleries that opened in the Autumn of 1993. On the same floor are the Islamic and Oriental Departments, the Hagop Kevorkian Gallery of the Ancient Middle East, and exhibits of Greek, Roman and Coptic art. The Fine Arts are represented by a collection of Prints and Drawings and the museum's collections of European and American painting and sculpture. The Brooklyn Museum was one of the first American institutions to concern itself with interior design and furniture; their seventeenth- and eighteenth-century rooms first opened in 1929, the nineteenth-century period rooms in 1953.

In the Freda Schiff Warburg Sculpture Garden can be seen architectural fragments from Pennsylvania Station, which was pulled down in 1963 to the consternation of many New Yorkers, and Louis Sullivan's only New York project.

Address
200 Eastern Parkway
Brooklyn, N.Y. 11238
✆ (718) 638 5000

Map reference

How to get there
Subway: 2 and 3
Bus: B41, B48, B69 and B71.

Opening times
Wed to Sun, 10–5. Closed Mon and Tue.

Entrance fee
Suggested contribution of $4 adults; $2 students; $1.50 senior citizens. Free to members and children under 12 if accompanied by an adult.

Tours
Gallery talks at 2 every weekday. Weekend gallery talks at 2 and 3. To confirm call the number above. Group tours by appointment four weeks in advance.

Emblems of the Civil War

1888

Alexander Pope

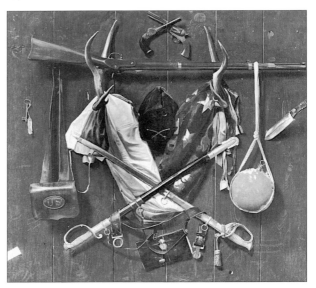

Still lives of *trompe l'oeil* memorabilia such as the present example were just one of several genres that Alexander Pope (1829–1924) tackled throughout his career. Pope's early paintings of animals earned him the title of 'American Landseer', and his later career was as a successful portraitist. It is probable that the artist first started producing still lives such as this in 1878, after the example of William Michael Harnett, whose hunting compositions had been highly acclaimed. However, this form of painting bears a curious relationship to portraiture since it celebrates, by means of weapons and insignia, the achievements of a particular individual, the Unionist Major General William Badger Tibbits, without ever describing his physical likeness. Tibbits' role in the Civil War of twenty-odd years before was long past, and the soldier himself had died eight years earlier at the age of forty-three. The rifles and sword form a vortex-like composition centred by Tibbits' cap hanging peak down on his regiment's flag. A sense of absence and nostalgia is summoned by this allusion to a flag-draped coffin. The inclusion of the antlers marks a parallel to hunting, long seen as a peaceable and gentlemanly 'dry-run' to battle. Tibbit's personal victory is commemorated by the water gourd and slightly battered hat, while any of the other objects, meticulously described, could refer to a symbolic and retrospective glorification of the Civil War.

The Peaceable Kingdom

c. 1840–1845

Edward Hicks

One of the most renowned naive painters of early nineteenth-century America, Edward Hicks (1780–1849) was apprenticed in 1801 to a coach maker as a painter of decorative panels. He later expanded his trade to encompass tavern and shop signs before becoming a Pennsylvania Quaker preacher in the early 1820s. The Brooklyn Museum's version of *The Peaceable Kingdom* is one of a hundred paintings of the same subject executed by Hicks between 1820 and his death in 1849. Rather than being commissioned or painted speculatively, they were illustrations of his ideal of spiritual life in America, and were either sold for very little money or given to friends as presents. The gathering of beasts and children in an arcadian landscape was based on the passage in the *Book of Isaiah* which prophesies the lion lying down with the lamb, an optimistic hope for religious tolerance in the new democracy. Some of the versions include a scene from William Penn's *Holy Experiment,* where he receives from the Indians, or Native Americans, the charter for Pennsylvania. This image was taken from prints of the same subject after Benjamin West, but Hicks also made free use of popular engravings as sources for motifs in his work.

The Turtle Pond

1898

Winslow Homer

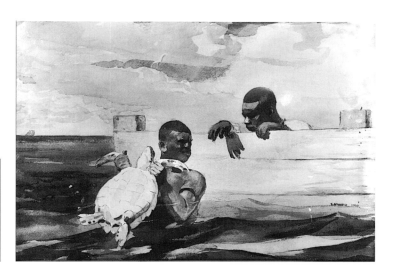

This was one of twenty-five paintings in watercolour executed by Homer (1836–1901) during two months spent in the Bahamas during the winter of 1898–99. Watercolour had recently been revived by an exhibition in 1873 promoted by the American Society of Painters in Watercolors. Here Homer, an artist who had achieved recognition as a magazine illustrator, can be seen to develop the full expressive range of that technique. The main figure is shown having caught a young sea turtle destined for the pound where it will be fattened before being sold. The artist describes a seemingly mundane moment which carries far deeper meanings about the captivity of man's existence, despite the idyllic tropical situation in which the two protagonists work.

The transparency of watercolour makes it a difficult medium with which to build tone and form, but Homer achieves a rich sense of solidity in the concrete elements of the scene; the men's anatomy, fencing and even the milky turtle. Yet at the same time he is able to retain the impression of the sea's translucency and the clouds' passing, while the paint maintains its own patterns and values on the paper. One instance of Homer's technical command can be seen in the shadow cast by the man standing within the pound. The hand itself is solid and convincing in its three-dimensionality, while the shadow it casts against the white fencing is flatter and just slightly more abstracted.

Hartley (1877–1948) was one of the artists in the circle of photographer and art dealer Alfred Stieglitz. It was in Stieglitz's gallery that he saw works by painters such as Cézanne, Matisse and Picasso two years before European modernism was to galvanize American painters at the 1914 Armory Show. Soon afterwards Stieglitz backed Hartley's departure for Paris, where he was swept up by the intellectual coterie surrounding Leo and Gertrude Stein. Through them he came into contact with contemporary German art, prompting his travels to Berlin in 1913. It was during this period that Hartley executed the series of pictures of which *Painting No. 48* is an outstanding example, which were inspired by the military spectacle he had witnessed at the eve of the World War One. Although the artist used a style derived from the Cubists to construct a hermetic picture space in which the elements vie with one another for pre-eminence, he differs from the Cubists in the highly significant imagery he uses. His letters to Stieglitz allude to the mystical properties of his motifs, such as numbers and shapes, revealing the influence of Kandinsky whom he admired, without really clarifying any one overall interpretation of the painting. However, given the historical context in which Hartley was working, his style does appear to evoke a visual, if not ideological fascination for the martial splendour of military parades; a love of the jostling, vivacious throng of helmets, braiding and insignia bristling in sunshine and optimism.

CATHEDRAL OF SAINT JOHN THE DIVINE

Begun 1892

Address
1047 Amsterdam Avenue at 112th Street, New York, NY 10026.
✆ (1) 31 67 400

Map reference
⑤

How to get there
Bus: 3, 4, 5, 18.
Subway: 1, 9.

Opening times
Open daily 7–5.

Entrance fee
$3. 00.

Tours
Tue–Sat at 11, Sun 12.45.

Saint John the Divine, the world's largest Gothic style church, was first planned as a Romanesque/ Byzantine cathedral in 1892 when the firm of Heins & La Farge won the commission for its construction over sixty other competitors. Construction proceeded slowly, so that by 1911 only the choir and the arches of the crossing had been erected. Eventually the Romanesque model was considered outdated, and in 1916 it was discarded. Instead, Ralph Adams Cram of Cram & Ferguson was hired to proceed in a Gothic style. The nave was finished by 1935, but construction on the north transept petered out, and with World War Two the whole project stopped until the 1960s when an abortive plan was conceived to complete the crossing in a contemporary style. By 1967 the Bishop announced the cessation of building in favour of social work for the surrounding neighbourhood. However, in 1978 the Trustees began fund-raising for the completion of the crossing and west facade. Work on the southwest tower began in 1982, and continues today. The stonemason's yard, where thirty local apprentices train with a master mason, can be visited.

Built 1960

The financial/civic space of the Plaza provides a dated, if ambitious marriage of corporate architecture and sculpture. The skyscraper (1960), designed by Skidmore, Owings & Merrill, was the first International Style tower to be built Downtown, and the pedestrian area in front of the building contains both Noguchi's *Japanese Garden*, (1960), and Dubuffet's *Group of Four Trees* (1972).

Isamu Noguchi (1904–89) was a Japanese-American sculptor influenced by both Eastern and Western traditions. The *Japanese Garden* is one of fourteen gardens he designed, intended to suggest an inspirational and calming mood at this hub of commerce, but the sunken cell also serves to supply light to the banking area beneath the Plaza. On the undulating mosaic surface of the basin are set rocks from the bed of the Uji River in Kyoto. The meditative qualities of Noguchi's *Garden* strike a very different chord to the energetic and somewhat caricatural flourishes of the *Group of Four Trees* by Jean Dubuffet (1901–85), which have been dubbed 'unleashed graphisms'.

Address
1 Chase Manhattan Plaza between Nassau and Liberty, William and Pine Streets, NewYork

Map reference

How to get there
Subway: 2, 3, 4, 5, A, C, J, M
Bus: M1, M6, M15

Opening times
Always open.

Entrance fee
Free.

Built 1930

Address
405 Lexington Avenue
between 42nd and 43rd
Streets, New York.

Map reference
⑦

How to get there
Subway: 4, 5, 6, 7, S.
Bus: M1, M2, M3, M4, M42,
M101, M102.

Opening times
During business hours.

Entrance fee
Free.

Much of the glory of the Chrysler Building derives from its modernity. Although built over sixty years ago its patron, the automobile tycoon Walter P. Chrysler, lavished the latest in design, materials and technology on the skyscraper by cladding its spire with gleaming stainless steel fashioned in rhythmic car motifs. The project for what remains the foremost Art Deco tower in New York was conceived by William H. Reynolds, a real estate speculator who aspired to build the tallest building in the world in partnership with the architect William Van Alen, but then sold the plans and lease to Chrysler in 1928. The dramatic completion of the building was inspired by Van Alen's acrimonious rivalry with H. Craig Severance, who seemed to have won in the height stakes with his building at 40 Wall Street. But just as the matter seemed settled, the Chrysler Building gained 121 feet when its spire emerged through a hole on the roof. It was for a short time the tallest building in New York and the world, but the completion of the Empire State Building in 1931 meant that it was soon overtaken.

The present Church of the Incarnation was largely rebuilt and expanded in 1882 when a fire damaged most of the original Neo-Gothic building. However, this was in many ways its making since the glory of this church rests on the windows installed during that refurbishment. A committee of parishioners from surrounding Murray Hill – at that time the richest area of Manhattan – replaced the windows with new stained glass from the best designers in America and England. On the north wall, two windows away from the altar, is the William Morris & Co.'s *Angels Commemorate All Infant Children*, installed next to a Tiffany composition showing *The Christian Pilgrim on the Road*. Also by the Tiffany Company are the massive doors below. The south wall begins with a window designed by Burne-Jones depicting *Faith and Charity* and continues with two more Tiffany windows: *Martha, Mary, and Jesus at the Tomb of Lazarus*, and *The Dignity of Labour*, to encompass a wide range of styles and motifs employed by glassmakers working within one decade of each other.

Address
207 Madison Avenue
Between 35th and 36th
Streets, New York.

Map reference

How to get there
Bus: M1, M2, M3, M4.

Opening times
Mon, Tues, Wed, Fri
11,30–2. Sunday service.

Entrance fee
Free.

CITY CENTER OF DRAMA AND MUSIC

Built 1924

Address
135 W 55, between 6th &
7th Avenues, New York.

Map reference

How to get there
Subway: B, D, F, Q, N, R.
Bus: M5, M6, M7.

Opening times
Not open to the public.

From 1943 the City Center served as the venue for both the New York City Ballet and the New York Opera until both companies relocated to the Lincoln Centre in the 1960s. However, this pseudo-Moorish hall was built for altogether different purposes. When it first opened in 1924 it was the Mecca Temple of the Ancient and Accepted Order of the Mystic Shrine, one of several Masonic Lodges which existed in New York in the 1920s. Sometimes known as the Shriners, Masons of all nationalities have long adopted the ceremonial of pantomime 'eastern' culture.

The facade of the building is covered in blocks of warm coloured sandstone, with the entrances picked out in tile-work bearing Islamic designs. The Moorish motif continues up to the top of the building, which is surmounted by a tiled and onion-shaped dome. Although the building is relatively unknown and somewhat overshadowed by neighbouring Broadway, it provides an example of the wide range of architectural forms, revived or original, to be found in this most concentrated of cities.

Of all the monuments that punctuate the landscape of Central Park, Cleopatra's Needle is the most famous, not only because of its antiquity, but also due to the focal position it occupies at the centre of the park. The sixteenth-century BC. obelisk was presented to the City of New York in 1877 by the Khedive Ishmail Pasha of Egypt, and is inscribed with hieroglyphics commemorating the achievements of King Thutmes, Son of the Sun. Much of the impetus behind its importation was the idea that New York could not consider itself a world capital until it had an obelisk such as those in the Old World. As an article in the *New York Herald* put it: 'It would be absurd for the people of any great city to hope to be happy without an Egyptian Obelisk. Rome has had them this great while and so has Constantinople. Paris has one. London has one. If New York was without one, all those great sites might point the finger of scorn at us and intimate that we could never rise to any real moral grandeur until we had our obelisk.' The installation of the obelisk next to the Metropolitan Museum was seen as a way of supporting it as the future national gallery of America.

Address
Central Park, behind the Metropolitan Museum of Art, New York.

Map reference
 ⑩

How to get there
Subway: 4, 5, 6.
Bus: M1, M2, M3, M4.
Enter Central Park by 79th Street entrance.

Address
Fort Tryon Park, New York
✆ 212 923 3700

Map reference
⑪

How to get there
Subway: A
Bus: M4, M98

Opening times
Tue to Sun 9.30–5.15.

Entrance fee
$ 7 adults. $3.50 senior
citizens and students.
Children under 12 free if
accompanied by an adult.

Tours
3.00 daily.

The Cloisters, a branch of The Metropolitan Museum, displays a wide range of medieval art in a neo-monastic context that is suggested as much by the original architectural fragments as the 1930s building or its romanticized setting. The core of the collection was first formed by George Grey Barnard, the sculptor who opened a museum of the medieval objects he had collected and imported to New York on the eve of World War One. Barnard's Cloisters, to distinguish them from The Cloisters, were arranged in a more theatrical manner than the present museum, with the guards dressed as monks and the exhibits illuminated by torchlight. By 1925 the impoverished Barnard had succeeded in selling his museum to the Metropolitan, supported by John D. Rockefeller Jr.. Rockefeller not only financed the construction of the museum – based on a generalized monastic plan – but also its picturesque situation. This involved the purchase and landscaping of Fort Tryon Park, and that of the Palisades National Park so as to preserve an unblemished view across the Hudson.

Rockefeller's first suggestions for the museum involved a castellated structure based on models such as Kenilworth Castle. However, he was steered away from this by the first Curator, James Lorimer, who was largely responsible for the design of the museum as it is today.

The integration of medieval architecture with the 1930s museum makes for the most spectacular aspect of The Cloisters. Of the five cloisters incorporated into the museum, the central and most renowned is the one reconstructed from elements first built in the mid-twelfth century at Cuxa in the Pyrenees. Furthermore, the installations of three of the cloisters have provided opportunities for three thematic gardens which illustrate the importance of horticulture in the Middle Ages. For example, the Trie-en-Bigorre Cloister contains examples of plants used for symbolic reasons which are illustrated in the last of the *Unicorn Tapestries*.

THE CLOISTERS

A relatively late addition to The Cloisters, this twelfth-century Romanesque apse was added to the collection and structure of the museum in 1957. It was once part of a fortified hill-town located seventy-five miles north of Madrid, and the narrowness of its lancet windows reveals the defensive aspects of the chapel's design. After it had fallen out of use as a church the apse remained the only standing part of the chapel, and it was used as a sheltered cemetery for the Fuentidueñan citizens. The monumentality of the structure is broken up by sculptural elements such as the figures of St. Martin to the left, and immediately opposite, *The Annunciation*. On the capitals of the foremost columns are found smaller narrative scenes; on the left *The Adoration of the Magi*, and on the right *Daniel in the Lion's Den*. The two decorative holes in the back wall of the apse originally served as shelves for the liturgical objects used during the mass. The Byzantine-style fresco showing the *Enthroned Madonna and Child* was placed here only in 1957. Contemporary with the apse, it originates from the same region of northern Spain, and shows the Virgin dominating the space, with the less significant figures of the archangels Gabriel and Michael and the Magi relegated to a smaller scale. The apse, which is on permanent loan from the Spanish government, is used for medieval music performances held each winter.

1425

Robert Campin

THE CLOISTERS

Whereas the *Unicorn Tapestries* are The Cloisters' foremost examples of courtly art, this little altarpiece by Campin (1378/9–1444) was commissioned by a Flemish merchant. He has been identified as Inglebrecht of Mechelen who had business interests in Tournai, Bruges and Malines, towns possibly seen in the backgrounds of the triptych. Inglebrecht and his wife are shown in the left wing in attitudes of devotion witnessing Gabriel's announcement to the Virgin Mary. The interior is contemporary and contains furnishings and objects that would have been familiar to the painter and his audience. The miraculous nature of Christ's birth is here illustrated according to St. Bernard's description of the Incarnation where the tiny spirit of Christ – already aware of His death as he carries a cross – flies in through a window, marking the moment at which He was immaculately conceived. The third panel of the triptych also refers to Christ as Redeemer by showing Joseph at work making mousetraps. The symbolism of the mousetrap was described by St. Augustine who equated the cross with a trap for the Devil, and Christ's death as his bait.

The naturalism of this painting is due in great part to Campin's use of the recently discovered technique of oil painting. The slow-drying medium allowed him to use tiny brushes for intricate details and a wide range of textures and light effects.

The scarcity of documents relating to these tapestries has meant that no one understanding of their origin or meaning can be satifactorily reached. However, it seems likely that they convey an allegory that parallels the story of Christ's Passion. In the second tapestry twelve perplexed huntsmen gather around the fountain where the Unicorn dips his horn into the water so as to rid him of a serpent, symbol of satanic evil. This scene could be read as referring to the Last Supper. In the fifth tapestry the death of the Unicorn is comparable to Christ's crucifixion, as the mythical beast is lanced in the side, and he wears a crown of thorns around his neck. In the last scene (shown above) the Unicorn, representing the Resurrected Christ, is shown in a paradisical garden, looking heavenward.

THE CLOISTERS

The Cloisters Cross
Mid-12th century

For many years thought to have been an altar cross from the Abbey of Bury St. Edmunds, this intricately carved object is made up of seven pieces of walrus ivory. From the holes on the front of the cross it has been deduced that a figure of the crucified Christ is missing. However, all the remaining parts refer to His sacrifice: against the front of the crucifix is carved The Tree of Life, and at the end of each arm an episode of Christ's Death and Resurrection, with His Ascension placed at the top. The central medallion depicts Moses and the Brazen Serpent, used as an Old Testament prefiguration of the Crucifixion, and at the base figures of Adam and Eve are shown grasping the cross as acknowledgment of its power against Original Sin.

THE CLOISTERS

THE COOPER-HEWITT MUSEUM

Address
2 East 91st Street
New York, N.Y. 10128
✆ 212 860 6868

Map reference
⑫

How to get there
Subway: 4, 5, and 6
Bus: M1, M2, M3, M4, M18,
and M19.

Opening times
Tue 10–9; Wed to Sat 10–5;
Sun 12–5; closed Mon.

Entrance fee
$3 adults. $1.50 for
students over 12 and senior
citizens. Members and
younger children admitted
free.

Tours
Tue 4 and 7.30; Wed 11 and
2; Thur 1 and 3; Fri at 2; Sat
at 1. For further information
and disabled access call
number above.

The Cooper-Hewitt is the Smithsonian Institution's National Museum of Design, housed in the mansion of Andrew Carnegie, former telegraph boy and later steel magnate. The building dates from 1901 and was designed by Babb, Cook & Willard. Carnegie's request for 'the most modest, plainest, and roomiest house in New York' was fulfilled in the sixty-four rooms of the house. The design of red brick trimmed with decorative details in limestone, known as Neo-Georgian, is neither under-stated nor simple.

A canopy of stained glass and copper shelters the front door, from which one enters a marble vestibule and rich oak-panelled Great Hall. This gives accesss to what were public rooms such as the Music Room and Garden Vestibule (where the windows were designed by Tiffany), Dining Room and Breakfast Room; these are now used as gallery space to show revolving exhibitions based on a rich and wide-ranging collection of design and applied arts. The rooms of the second floor are also used for exhibiting the collection on a rotating basis and include the former Billiard Room, Library and bedrooms. What were the servant's quarters now house the Drue Heinz Study Center for Drawings and Prints. The 3,000 prints and drawings in the collection relate primarily to architecture, design and ornament. In addition the museum owns fine examples of china, glass, furniture, woodwork, jewellery, metalwork and textiles.

The idea of a museum dedicated to design was first suggested to Sarah, Eleanor and Amy Hewitt, the granddaughters of Peter Cooper, by the Victoria and Albert Museum in London and the Musée des Art Décoratifs in Paris. The core of the permanent collection was opened to the public in 1897 as the Cooper Union Museum for the Arts of Decoration. In 1963 the Cooper-Union ceased to operate as such for lack of funds, but was soon rescued by its incorporation with the Smithsonian.

The Dia Center for the Arts (known as the Dia Art Foundation until 1990) was established in 1974 by the German art collector Heine Friedrich and his wife Philippa de Menil for the purpose of supporting contemporary art which, because of its nature or scale, could not be accommodated by conventional museums. Most of the money for the center, and the art projects it sponsors, derives from the De Menil fortune which was established in the Texas oil boom of the later 1960s and 1970s. The De Menils were responsible for patenting an indispensable component to oil drills, used throughout the world in petroleum wells. Since 1987, Dia has occupied a warehouse building which shows year-long site-specific installations of contemporary art. The forms of contemporary art which are commissioned and collected by the Dia encompass the most important movements of the post-war period. Most significantly, Dia and the De Menils were responsible for backing many of the Land Art projects of recent years, including undertakings of vast ambition and expense such as Walter de Maria's *Lightning Field* of 1974.

Across the street from the current exhibition space Dia is renovating another warehouse building which will serve as a museum devoted to the permanent collection of art from the 1960s and 1970s, including work by Joseph Beuys, Donald Judd, Barnett Newman, Cy Twombly and Andy Warhol. The recently inaugurated Andy Warhol Museum in Pittsburg was supported by the Dia who gave a considerable number of works from their collection.

Other satellites of the Dia include a 3,500 square-foot room at 141 Wooster Street in which Walter de Maria's *New York Earth Room* is on permanent display. Also by De Maria is the *Broken Kilometer*, five rows of one hundred parallel brass columns arranged in the Dia premises at 393 West Broadway.

Address
548 West 22nd Street
New York, N.Y. 10011
✆ 212 989 5912

Map reference

How to get there
Subway: C and E
Bus: M23, and M11.

Opening times
Thur to Sun 12–6. Closed
Mon to Wed and during
July and August.

Entrance fee
Free.

EMPIRE STATE BUILDING

Built 1931

Address
350 Fifth Avenue. 34th Street between 5th and 6th Streets, New York

Map reference

How to get there
Subway: B, D, F, N, R, 1,2,6 and 9.
Bus: M1, M2, M3, M4, M5, M18.

Opening times
Daily 9.30–11.30 p.m.

Entrance fee
Free admission to Lobby. View from 86th and 102nd floors $3.75 adults, $1.75 under 12 years.

As one of the skyscrapers caught up in the race for tallest building in New York, the verticality of the Empire State Building informs its appearance as much as any other aspect. After sixteen projected designs the team of Shreve, Lamb and Harmon arrived at a solution that is as monumental as it is vertiginous. All eighty-six storeys are unified into a pattern of soaring modernity by the stainless steel mullions that are set out from the glass and limestone curtain walls. The building was constructed with unprecedented speed and efficiency at a rate of four-and-a-half floors a week; it took less time and money to complete than predicted. Once the top floor and seemingly the whole project was finished the backers felt that more emphasis at the summit of the building was needed, and so in 1929 the extra 150 feet were supplied by a zeppelin mooring mast. Despite the technological ambition behind this final addition, it never served its function, and remains more famous in the iconography of New York as the site of King Kong's death.

Built 1902

The impact of the Flatiron, or Fuller Building (named after its builder) is largely based on the peculiarities of urban planning in New York. The distinctive triangular plan of the building was dictated by its site at the junction of Fifth Avenue and Broadway, where the famous rectilinear street grid is disrupted by Broadway's diagonal transection of the city from 106th Street down to 10th. The Flatiron Building remains an early example of steel frame construction in New York, but despite the technological advances of this form of engineering, architects such as D. H. Burnham were reluctant at first to match the modernity of the structure to that of the design. The motifs of the exterior terracotta cladding are all traditional, so that the most revolutionary aspect of the building remains the view from its six-foot wide, or rather narrow point, as it splays back. This radical departure from the block or tower format of most Manhattan constructions inspired some of the most atmospheric photography – by Edward Steichen, for example – that is known of the city.

Address
949 Broadway at 23rd Street, New York, NY 10011.

Map reference
(15)

How to get there
Subway: R, N.
Bus: M2, M3, M5, M6, M7, M23.

Opening times
Lobby open to the public during office hours.

Address
62 5th Avenue
New York, N.Y. 10011
✆ 212 206 5549

Map reference
(16)

How to get there
Subway: 1, 2, 3, 4, 5, 6, B, F, L, N, Q, R, and S.
Bus: M2, M3, M5, M6, and M14.

Opening times
Tue to Sat, 10–4. Thurs by appointment only.
Closed Sun and Mon.

Entrance fee
Free.

Tours
By arrangement.

The Forbes Magazine Galleries opened in 1985 to display the eclectic and eccentric collection of Malcolm S. Forbes, magazine publisher and billionaire. The gallery is housed in a building designed by Carrère & Hastings – architects of the Frick and New York Public Library – and built by Harold MacMillan before he entered political life. Forbes began collecting while still at Princeton. His initial purchase in 1937 was a note written by President Abraham Lincoln, the first item of a rare and extraordinary corpus of presidential papers and memorabilia including the glasses Lincoln was using on the night of his assassination. Although the most renowned part of the collection is the Fabergé Room containing twelve bejewelled Easter eggs made between 1885 and 1916 for the Imperial Russian court, the greater part of the gallery's exhibits are made up of the toy boats and toy soldiers of which Forbes was such a keen collector. Some of these form historical vignettes such as the ceremonial procession celebrating Anthony and Cleopatra, or sentimental groups such as *Home Farm*, an anti-war toy advocating conscientious objection from World War One.

A by no means insignificant part of the Forbes collection comprises paintings by Matisse, Reynolds, Gainsborough, Hopper, Benton and Bellows, although these may not all be on show at once since paintings are displayed in constantly changing exhibitions. Forbes's love of images associated with power and worldliness also led him to collect French nineteenth-century military paintings and to assemble a room full of trophies. As Forbes saw it, 'This trophy room is a moving reminder that all things and all of us are too soon over and out'. However, the prizes displayed here are not exclusively about grand achievement and include ephemeral and humble items such as the trophy for the best chickens at the Northamptonshire Egg Laying Trials in 1929–30.

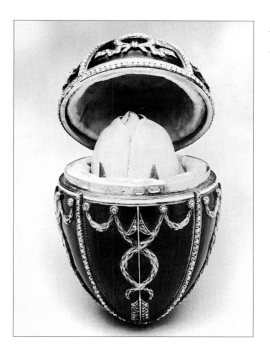

The most featured aspect of the Forbes Magazine Collection is its 300 decorative objects by Fabergé, including the largest surviving group of Imperial Easter eggs. Fabergé was the court jeweller to Czars Alexander III and Nicholas II between 1885 and 1916, for whom his workshop of almost 500 craftsmen made fifty-four Easter eggs. Of these, forty-five are known to exist today, twelve of which are in the Forbes Collection. The eggs and other spectacular trinkets such as a silver music box in the shape of a paddle steamer, allow some idea of the lavishness of Russian court life in the thirty-one years before the Revolution. Aside from the splendour of the individual eggs, the advantage of seeing them grouped together is that the great range of motifs, decoration and technical inventiveness of the different variations can be seen and compared.

As an elaborate manifestation of Russian Orthodox tradition, the Czars followed the custom of presenting Easter eggs to their wives and mothers. For Easter 1895 Czar Nicholas gave his wife Alexandra the Imperial Rosebud Egg. The exterior of the egg is covered in red enamel with chased gold appliqué in a pattern of swags and bows; a sumptuous if somewhat formal decoration which sets up the surprise of a yellow enamelled rosebud inside. The rosebud has a lever on its side which allows the bud to bloom and reveal a minuscule portrait of the Czar.

⊛ Four Seasons Hotel

Built 1993

Address
57th Street between
Madison and Park Avenues,
New York

Map reference
⑰

How to get there
Subway: 4, 6, E, F.

Opening times
Open at all times.

Entrance fee
Free.

The Four Seasons is the most recent skyscraper and the tallest hotel to be built in Manhattan. Consciously and self-consciously luxurious, it was lavishly designed by I.M. Pei in an eclectic style that harks back to the great Art Moderne towers of the 1920s and 1930s. A quality of monumental drama is achieved by the limestone cladding, crisply cut into geometric forms on the facade. The public grandiosity of the building is set by its large central doorway, flanked by six narrow lateral openings. The only curve of the exterior is supplied by a blind oculus hovering above the entrance, the width of which continues up the entire height of the building, gradually tapering until it reaches its summit at the fifty-second floor. The height of the tower is enhanced by seven setbacks which become gradually taller as it reaches its summit at 682 feet. Although relatively small at 367 rooms (costing roughly one million dollars each to build), Pei's ambitious scale for the building is set by the lobby where colossal columns rise to a thirty-three-foot-high onyx ceiling.

Although the mansion which houses the Frick Collection was commissioned in 1905 by Henry Clay Frick (1849–1919) as a private house, it was intended to protect and display Frick's collection. Frick, magnate of the coke industry, Chairman of the Carnegie Steel Corporation, and a director of U.S. Steel, began collecting in the late 1880s, mainly contemporary, academic French painters such as Bonheur and Bouguereau. At the turn of the century Frick's taste had become unfashionable and he began to buy English and Dutch Old Masters. Then from 1905, his collecting was mainly conducted through the offices of art dealers Lord Duveen, Roland Knoedler, and Charles Carstairs. Duveen's most important negotiations on behalf of Frick involved the purchase of decorative objects from J. P. Morgan's estate including Chinese and Limoges china and Renaissance bronzes. It was Duveen who influenced Frick to choose Thomas Hastings of Carrère & Hastings as his architect for the last mansion in New York to occupy a whole block, a lavish, expansive design influenced by French *hôtels* of the reign of Louis XVIII. The interiors, designed by the London firm of White Allom were derived from French and English eighteenth-century prototypes. Apart from the fine workmanship they provide, the interiors enable the paintings to be seen in a context which also complements the decorative arts in the collection; these are of as high a standard as Frick's pictures.

Frick intended to bequeath his collection to the public and accordingly the trust he left enabled a third of the collection to be added after his death. Ingres' *Comtesse de Haussonville* (page 48), for example, was bought by trustees rather than Frick.

Mrs. Frick lived until 1931 when John Russell Pope, on the suggestion of Lord Duveen, was engaged to make the necessary alterations to turn the house into a fully-fledged gallery. The house and collection were eventually opened to the public in 1935.

Address
1 East 70th Street
New York, N.Y. 10021

Map reference

How to get there
Subway: 6
Bus: M1, M2, M3, M3, M4, M29, and M30.

Opening times
Tue to Sat, 10–6 .
Sun 1–6. Closed Mon.

Entrance fee
$5 adults, $3 students and senior citizens.
Children under 10 not admitted.

Tours
Audio visual tours every hour on the half hour starting at 10:30.

The Four Seasons

1755

François Boucher

Of the sixteen paintings by Boucher (1703–70) bought by Frick, eleven panels make up the series of Arts and Sciences seen in the Boucher Room, one is the intimate little portrait of Madame Boucher reclining coquettishly in her boudoir, and the remaining four illustrate another aspect of the painter's decorative work. According to the set of engravings by Jean Daullé printed after Boucher's designs, *The Four Seasons* were executed for Louis XV's mistress, Madame de Pompadour, and more than likely were made to hang as overdoors, although it has not been established for which house or château they were intended. The lighthearted, pleasurable mood of these scenes in which the protagonists are shown enjoying seasonal pastimes in a pastoral mode is also supported by the inscriptions to Daullé's prints where they are described as *The Charms of Spring*, *The Pleasures of Summer*, *The Delights of Autumn* and *The Amusements of Winter*. At the Frick where the scenes hang in the West Vestibule, they have been framed as four little easel paintings and are displayed at eye level. It should be remembered, however, that they were designed to be seen from below, from which viewpoint their perspective and formal design make most sense.

The eleven scenes depicting *The Progress of Love* slip between several modes; decorative, narrative and allegorical, to trace a sequence through a subject favoured by many patrons of the Ancien Régime. Starting with *The Pursuit*, the canvases continue clockwise around the room with *Love Letters*, *Love the Avenger*, *Love the Sentinel*, *Hollyhocks*, *Love the Jester*, *Reverie*, *Love Triumphant*, *The Lover Crowned*, *The Meeting*, and *Love Pursuing a Dove*. Four of the eleven can be traced back to 1771 when Madame du Barry, the mistress of Louis XV, commissioned them to hang in a new garden pavilion at her château at Louveciennes. However, she eventually rejected them in favour of another series painted by Joseph-Marie Vien for reasons that have not been established, although it has been suggested that the resemblance to the King and his mistress of the central characters offended Louis XV. Another possibility is that the sobriety of Vien's style was more appropriate to the Neoclassical design of the pavilion.

In 1790 Fragonard (1732–1806) took the rejected paintings to Grasse, where he had them installed in his cousin's house with the additional seven scenes. The stagey dramatism of the paintings relates them to pictorial traditions first established by Watteau of Commedia dell'Arte-inspired sagas enacted in grand Italianate gardens. Although lush and exuberant, the plants and flowers serve to frame and emphasize the stages of seduction, and the attitudes of the statues provide knowing commentaries on the human foibles they witness.

1480–85
Giovanni Bellini

Giovanni Bellini (*c.* 1430/40–1516) was among the first painters in Venice to use oil paint, a slow-drying medium which enabled him to render landscapes that were at once detailed and atmospheric. The wide range of tones and light effects that can be achieved with oil facilitated Bellini's representation of a glowing landscape in which resonant sunshine implies the presence of God as much as St. Francis's rapt meditation. The precise subject of the picture has been much disputed, but a possible reading is that it shows St. Francis receiving the stigmata while on retreat to Mount Averna, which would account for his outstretched hands and extended foot. However, other aspects of the saint's life are alluded to, for example his renunciation of earthly goods.

As in contemporary Flemish paintings – which were admired by the Venetians of Bellini's circle – casual references to the minutiae of everyday life are seen in the simple sandals, desk and book that St. Francis has walked away from to commune with God. Similarly he has left behind the skull, to acknowledge the redemptive power of Christ. The love of nature and animals with which the saint is most widely associated is presented here as complementary to his transcendental experience of the miracle.

Holbein's depiction of Sir Thomas More, humanist scholar and Lord Chancellor of England under Henry VIII, lends a private, psychological intensity to the state portrait. When Holbein (1497–1543) first arrived in England in 1526 he stayed with More, his first patron, who was in contact with German humanist circles. Foremost amongst these was Erasmus whose treatise *In Praise of Folly* prompted More to write *Utopia* in response. The portrait dates from 1527 when More held the position of Speaker of the House of Commons. The chain of office he wears was added after he was made Chancellor in 1529. A loyal Catholic, More would not go along with the King's attempts to divorce Catherine of Aragon. His refusal to swear allegiance to the new law of succession led to his resignation and eventual execution for high treason in 1535.

In this portrait, for which there are two preparatory drawings at Windsor, More is presented as a public figure in state regalia, holding a document of state. His concentrated gaze away from the spectator allows us an unguarded insight into his meditative personality. Holbein directs attention to More's face by highlighting it against the rich, dense tones and textures of the fur and velvet cloak. The careful description of lines and shadows formed by More's facial expression alludes to a thoughtful and considered character. In this respect Holbein follows the traditions of evocative, intimate portraits established by Raphael and Titian

The sitter for this sumptuous, captivating, but formal portrait by Ingres (1780–1867) was Louise, Princesse de Broglie, the twenty-seven-year-old granddaughter of Madame de Staël. Ingres' account of its completion reveals a degree of cynicism about its reception: 'I finished that disastrous portrait which, weary of tormenting me has had four days of private exhibition in my studio and has brought me the most complete success.' It had taken three years to complete, and nine days to paint one of her hands. This considerable effort produced an image of studied casualness; the Comtesse is shown in her private sitting room, assuming a pose of graceful insouciance. Much of the cool and rarefied air of the painting is achieved by Ingres' use of blue tones which predominate and tie the many details together. On the mantelpiece can be seen notes and personal effects, such as the pair of binoculars. A degree of intimacy is also achieved by the device of placing the sitter against a mirror in which the back of her head, elaborate hair dressing and neck are reflected.

Raphael was Ingres' foremost influence and in this portrait he makes several references to the *Madonna della Sedia* in the Pitti Palace, Florence. Both show the subjects posed with an intimate placement of the arms around the body, the head gently tilted to one side. In 1514, as in 1845, oriental fashions were highly prized, and just as Raphael's Madonna is seen in a turban and paisley shawl, Louise de Haussonville wears exotic gold and turquoise jewellery, and her paisley-hemmed shawl is casually thrown over the arm of the chair on the right.

From 1620 Velázquez (1599–1660) worked almost exclusively as court painter to the Hapsburg King of Spain, Philip IV. There remain portraits of Philip by Velázquez relating to practically every stage and aspect of his reign. As with the *Equestrian Portrait of Philip IV* in the Prado in Madrid, here Velázquez depicts the King as a martial, but highly ceremonial figure. The reference to battle is specific. The latter years of Philip's rule were blighted by his struggles to keep the Bourbons in France from assimilating Spain into their growing empire, but he had recently scored an important tactical victory at the Battle of Fraga. Philip is seen wearing the battle dress of his triumph, holding a tricorne in one hand and a baton in the other. In this respect Velázquez makes an oblique reference to Titian's 1554 *Portrait of Charles V* (also in the Prado); Philip's grandfather, who is also seen commemorating a victory, wears lavish armour and holds a baton, as did the Roman emperors in their triumphant displays. The ornate fabric and embroidery of the uniform is described in detail, but also with the free, rich, painterly style that he developed towards the latter half of his career. The elaborate play of silver thread and braiding against the pink silk mark a striking difference to the sober black dress that was favoured by the Spanish court and in which the King was more usually portrayed.

The Rehearsal

1878–79

Edgar Degas

In his work Degas (1834–1917) displayed a lifelong concern for specialized forms of movement as revealed by his paintings of racehorses, musicians, laundresses, milliners, and of course ballet dancers. This canvas is thought to be the painting entitled *Ecole de Danse* that was shown in the Fourth Impressionist Exhibition of 1879. Despite the outbreak of World War One it was bought by Frick, a rare modern work for him, in 1914.

There are two types of movement seen here, each dependent on the other, but quite self-contained. In the bottom left corner the violinist who accompanies the dancers gazes out of the picture plane, seemingly unaware of their routine. Degas has made a study of the different play of the musician's hands, the nearer one tilted limply downwards as he draws the bow across the violin, whereas his other hand is upturned into a complex arrangement, holding down the strings. The concentration of the dancers shows itself very differently; even in rehearsal their faces display the fixed smiles of the forthcoming performance. Degas uses the brilliant splashes of yellow, pink and blue provided by their tights, bows and collars to introduce colour into the bare and sun-bleached room. His interest in a ceremonial and specialized form of movement was also a feature of the Japanese prints he loved and collected, and in *The Rehearsal* he adopts a technique often used by Japanese artists of cutting some parts of the subject with the frame to create a sense of immediacy as the spectator seems to 'happen' on the scene.

Built 1913

Grand Central Station was planned by Cornelius Vanderbilt, the transportation mogul. By 1903 his chief engineer, William J. Wilgus had conceived a system of two levels of submerged rail and looping track, enabling trains to turn without backing out of the station. The architectural design (1913) was supplied by two firms: Reed and Stem, and Warren and Wetmore, who were largely responsible for the grandiose Main Concourse. This vast area is vaulted with an elliptical roof, influenced by Roman Baths. It is covered in marble and artificial Caen stone to contrast with the brilliant blue ceiling decorated with patterns based on the constellations. The south facade is dominated by Jules-Félix Coutan's vast clock (1912–14) surrounded by Hercules to represent physical energy, Minerva for intellectual energy, and at the top Mercury, embodying speed, traffic and the transmission of intelligence. The setting of this Beaux-Arts sculpture with such Futurist sentiments against the International Style Met Life Building bears testimony to the financial survival of the station. It was the first building in Manhattan to capitalize on its own air rights.

Address
42nd Street between Vanderbilt Avenue and Park Avenue, New York

Map reference

How to get there
Subway: 4, 5, 6, 7, S.
Bus: M1, M2, M3, M4, M18, M42, M101, M102.

Opening times
At all times.

Entrance fee
Free.

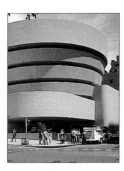

Address
1071 Fifth Avenue at 88th
Street
New York, N.Y. 10128
✆ 212 423 3500

Map reference

How to get there
Subway: 4, 5, or 6
Bus: M1 M2 M3, M4.

Opening times
Sun to Wed 10–6; Fri and
Sat 10–8. Closed Thur.

Entrance charge
$7 adults; $4 students and
senior citizens.

Tours
6.30 on Tues; 2.30 Wed to
Sun.

The Collections

Initially, the collection of Solomon R. Guggenheim (1861–1949) resembled those of many of his peers and consisted mainly of Old Master paintings. The pattern of his aquisition changed in the late 1920s due to the influence and direction of his friend, the German painter Baroness Hilla Rebay von Ehrenwiesen, who introduced the mining magnate to her circle of modernist artists including Kandinsky, Léger, Delaunay, Gleizes, and Chagall. The Baroness subsequently became the first director of the Solomon R. Guggenheim Collection of Non-Objective Painting at 24 East 54th Street, and it was she who suggested Frank Lloyd Wright as architect of the new building. In 1949 Guggenheim died and Hilla Rebay resigned three years later. The scope of the museum changed under her successor, James Johnson Sweeney, who from 1952 directed the collection towards figurative art by purchasing works by Picasso and Cézanne. He also began acquiring sculpture which Rebay had shunned. A later bequest of Impressionist and Post-Impressionist works by the dealer Justin K. Thanhauser in 1965 further distanced the brief of the museum from pure abstraction.

In 1979 on the death of Guggenheim's niece, Peggy, her remarkable collection of Surrealist and abstract painting and sculpture was added to the jurisdiction of the museum, but from a distance, since Peggy Guggenheim's collection remains in the Palazzo Venier dei Leoni in Venice where she lived. Over 300 Minimalist works were added to the collection in 1990 when the museum acquired paintings and sculptures owned by Count and Countess Panza di Biumo, who have also promised their villa near Milan to the Guggenheim. Following an extensive programme of expansion completed in 1992, the main space of the museum, arranged along the ramps, is used for temporary exhibitions with the permanent collections housed on the several floors of the annexe.

The Guggenheim is Frank Lloyd Wright's only building in New York and differs from much of his domestic architecture in its centralized form. The spiral design is reflected on the exterior as a type of inverted, circular ziggurat, while on the inside a continuous ramp a quarter of a mile long rises up towards a central skylight, allowing a progressive view of the paintings hung on the walls.

Wright considered his design to be organic, and maintained a formal unity between the whole of the building and its smaller parts by adapting all additional floors and window grilles to match the circular motif.

The museum took sixteen years to execute with the disruptions of World War Two, Guggenheim's death in 1949, and Wright's wrangles with Sweeney. Wright's death in 1959 came six months before the building opened to the public, so in 1968 it was his son-in-law, William Wesley Peters, who completed the annexe that Wright had first projected twenty years earlier. The 1990 programme of renovation, including the eleven-storey annexe that replaces Peter's version, provides more space for display of the collection.

Red Lily Pads

1956

Alexander Calder

The first excursion that the American Alexander Calder (1898–1976) made into sculpture was a busy, comic wire circus created in the 1920s, which can be seen on permanent display in the lobby of the Whitney Museum of American Art. Through a career of six decades Calder went on to work in other media and modes, experimenting also in drawings and paintings, but his Minimalist mobiles remain the most renowned area of his work. Some of Calder's mobiles are purely formal exercises in shape, colour, movement, and space, but this piece and several others suggest implicit or explicit subjects. Occasionally Calder would motorize the sculptures, but increasingly he came to rely on currents of air to gently propel the pieces which took on different compositions as they shifted. Here the floating motion of the mobile in air alludes to the same patterns traced on a pond's surface. The setting of the circular well of the Guggenheim museum provides a perfect context for the red discs of Calder's composition which can be seen from the various angles provided by Frank Lloyd Wright's spiraling ramps. From a vantage point above the sculpture the mobile is juxtaposed against the oval fountain at the base of the cell, and depending on the light effects, casts reflective tones on the water below.

Study for Composition II

1909–10

Wassily Kandinsky

The majority of art historians agree that this early work by Kandinsky (1866–1944) was a study for a larger composition in the Berlin collection of Baron von Gamp which was destroyed during World War Two. Although the content has been interpreted by some as a scene of The Deluge, and by others as The Garden of Love, any literal reading of the subject matter was side-stepped by Kandinsky who explained the work as an expression of inner feeling: 'It became the great ambition of my life to paint a Composition. They appear before me in my dreams – indistinct and fragmentary. Visions, sometimes frightening in their clarity. Sometimes I saw whole paintings, but when I awoke only the vaguest details, a faint trace remained. Once when I lay sick with typhoid fever I visualized an entire painting with great clarity. But when the fever had left me, it somehow crumbled in my memory.' One of the first painters to move away from objective representation, Kandinsky painted this lyrical but elusive scene while living in Munich as an exile from Russia. The Guggenheim owns eighteen paintings by Kandinsky, part of the core collection of non-objective art assembled during the 1920s and 1930s.

Merz 163

1941

Kurt Schwitters

For Schwitters, the majority of his work, be it paintings, collages, poems or buildings, was *Merz* of some form or other. He took the name from an advertisement for Kommerz-und Privat-Bank which he used in one of the many collages that make up his oeuvre. These could range from Merz environments such as the Merzbau he assembled on three floors of his house in Hanover, and then emulated in subsequent residences in Norway and England, to the elegant little collages of which this is an example. The material for Merz was always collected from the streets, but composed into images of unparalleled elegance in which the scraps harmonize with one another, either by means of shape, colour, texture or meaning.

Self Portrait

1980

Robert Mapplethorpe

The Guggenheim opened the most recent gallery of its new annexe in 1993, named after the photographer Robert Mapplethorpe (1946–89). Mapplethorpe's work was consistently figurative and ranged from the formal, staged portraits of friends and aquaintances in his Bohemian circle to extraordinarily graphic homoerotic images recorded with an incongruously cool style. The crisp and objective effect of Mapplethorpe's photographs relies in great part on his use of black and white in which the background is reduced to a white field, allowing a concentrated study of the subject, in which texture plays a large part. Despite this somewhat detatched approach the collected images of Mapplethorpe's career allow a sense of the turbulent play between the public and private aspects of his life. This can be traced most clearly in his self portraits.

The Hispanic Society of America forms part of a complex of cultural institutions conceived by Archer Milton Huntington in 1904. Huntington, son of the transportation magnate Collis P. Huntington, commissioned his nephew, Charles Pratt Huntington, to design the majority of the buildings which occupy land from the estate of John James Audubon, the painter and ornithologist. The sculptures found in the court in front of the museum are works by Huntington's wife, Anna Hyatt Huntington, including the bronze equestrian statue of *El Cid* dating from 1927.

Archer M. Huntington's interest in the culture of Spain and Portugal was formed when he travelled to Spain at the age of twenty-two. The collection, which opened in 1908, encompasses a range of objects from prehistoric fragments to art of the twentieth century displayed in the Main Court, adjoining corridor and Sorolla Room to the west. The collection is also rich in decorative arts including textiles, brocaded velvets, silks, laces and embroideries, metalwork, glass, ceramics, and furniture.

The Main Court, designed in Spanish Renaissance style, contains the paintings, sculpture, religious and decorative objects of the Society's collection, on both the ground floor and balcony of the mezzanine. The foremost artists of seventeenth-century Spain are represented; Velázquez, Zubarán, Murillo, and Goya. In the South Room can be seen works ranging from the fifteenth to seventeenth centuries, as well as the imposing Père Espalargues altarpiece dating from 1490. Eighteenth- and nineteenth-century tiles and glazed work from Valencia and Toledo are displayed in the corridor, and modern Spain is represented by murals of regional Spanish festivals by Joaquín Sorolla y Bastida in the Sorolla Room of 1911.

Address
Audubon Terrace
Broadway at 155th Street
New York, N.Y. 10032
✆ (212) 9262234

Map reference
㉑

How to get there
Subway: 1, B & K
Bus: M4, M5, M100 & M101

Opening times
Tue to Sat 10-4.30;
Sun 1–4. Closed Mon.

Entrance fee
Free.

Tours
Group tours by
appointment.

The Duchess of Alba

1797

Francisco de Goya

The portrait of the *Duchess of Alba* in the collection of the Hispanic Society was painted while Goya (1746–1828) was staying with her on her estate near Sanlúcar de Barrameda in southern Spain. It was there that the Duchess had retreated after her husband's death in June the previous year. A fashionable black beauty patch is visible at her right temple, but despite her elaborate costume the Duchess is represented wearing mourning dress. Goya has introduced his signature into the portrait by writing *Solo Goya*, or 'Goya alone' on the sand, to which the Duchess points, and *Goya* appears on one of her rings. *Alba* is inscribed on the one worn next to it. These details imply a certain intimacy felt for the Duchess by Goya, although it is said that his love for her was not reciprocated. The lore of Goya's life and career has promoted the Duchess of Alba as the sitter (or rather recliner) of the *Maja Naked* and the *Maja Clothed*, the two paintings of 1803–05 in the Prado, Madrid, which are said to portray the Duchess lying on a chaise longue, one in naked glory, the other more properly, but just as provocatively, dressed.

A sketch for the Hispanic Society's portrait survives as one of the sheets of Goya's Sanlúcar Album (now in the National Library of Madrid), a bound collection of drawings executed during his sojourn with the Duchess.

Camillo Astalli became Cardinal Pamphilj in 1650, on his adoption as cardinal-nephew to Pope Innocent x. Otherwise their only relationship was a vague kinship through the Pope's scheming sister-in-law, Donna Olympia Maidalchini. With the name Pamphilj also came the privilege of using the family palace in the Piazza Navona in Rome, and bearing the papal/princely coat of arms.

It remains a good measure of the artist's reputation that Velázquez (1599–1660) was so eagerly sought by the most influential patrons of Rome and the Curia during his second visit to Rome between 1648 and 1651. His intimate and gentle portrayal of Astalli must have been undertaken around the same time that he was working on the Pope's relentless, intense likeness (a painting which is still part of the Doria-Pamphilj collection in Rome). The rich, vivid range of reds used for this painting are enlived by a luminosity supplied by the white ground beneath the freely applied paint. X-ray examination of the canvas has revealed that the Cardinal was first shown wearing his beretta straight; the jaunty angle at which it is shown was a later alteration. The degree of weakness which characterizes Astalli's portrait – the submissive angle of his shoulders and the passive tilt of his chin – became clear with his downfall in 1654 when it was realized that Innocent's protégé was hopelessly incompetent. As rapidly as he had been promoted, he lost all claim to papal power.

Address
1109 Fifth Avenue
New York, N.Y., 10128
✆ (212) 423 3200

Map reference

How to get there
Subway: 6
Bus: M1, M2, M3, and M4.

Opening times
Sun, Mon, Wed, Thur
11–5:45. Tue 11–8. Closed
Fri, Sat and major legal and
Jewish holidays.

Entrance fee
$6 adults; $4 senior citizens
and students. Children
under 12 and museum
members free. Tues after 5
free to everyone.

The core of the collection of The Jewish Museum was established by Judge Mayer Sulzberger in 1904, as a part of the Jewish Theological Seminary. In 1944 the late Gothic-style mansion which houses the museum was donated to the seminary by Freda Schiff Warburg, the widow of the banker Felix Warburg. Designed by Cass Gilbert, the mansion was completed in 1908 and soon became renowned as one of the most elegant New York houses. The recent programme of modernization at the museum has expanded the available exhibition space and replaced a wing added in 1962. The architect Kevin Roche has followed, as far as possible, the original design of the Warburg mansion. Stonemasons from the team working at St. John the Divine assisted with the construction of the extension.

Dedicated to presenting the remarkable scope and diversity of Jewish culture, the Museum serves as a unique source of insight and inspiration for all people. Visitors enjoy an art experience which captures 4,000 years of Jewish life and culture. The Museum's permanent collection has grown to more than 27,000 objects – paintings, sculpture, works on paper, photographs, ethnographic material, archaeological artefacts, ceremonial objects and broadcast media materials – and is the largest and most comprehensive of its kind in the world. The centrepiece of the expanded museum is a two-floor permanent exhibition *Culture and Continuity: The Jewish Journey,* which conveys the essence of Jewish identity. This vibrant exhibition includes art, archaeology, audio and video displays, and an interactive computer programme on the Talmud. The Jewish Museum is also known for its temporary exhibitions, which often combine art and artefacts and interpret them through the lens of social history. These range from an exploration of pivotal historical events to the personal interpretation of Jewish culture by renowned contemporary artists such Rauschenberg and Johns.

Torah Ark from Westheim bei Hassfurt, Bavaria

c. 1725

Torah Arks such as this splendid eighteenth-century example are important for their religious, ceremonial and practical functions. They serve to protect and to some extent display the scrolls. These are hand-written by Torah scribes, and for them to remain kosher they cannot be damaged, hence the importance of keeping them locked away and safe. This example draws many cultural and aesthetic references from local examples of the Rococo, and the aedicule form of the Torah Ark echoes similar Neoclassical structures used for contemporary altarpieces. The lavish effects of marbles and gilded stuccoes are rendered here by means of richly painted pinewood. Above the aedicule are two lions rampant, a motif often used in heraldic imagery to signify balance, justice, order, and guardianship. The crown they hold is the Crown of Judah.

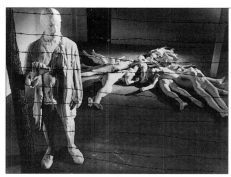

The Holocaust

1982

George Segal

The sculptural group of eleven life-size figures by George Segal (born 1924) is the plaster, wire and wood version of his bronze work located in San Francisco. Acquired by the museum in 1985, the setting of the group in a bleak unspecified indoor site serves to accentuate the desolation of the Holocaust. The burden of the survivor is acknowledged in the one isolated figure who turns his back on his fellow captives, all of whom are dead. The uniformity of the group, achieved by the lifeless white with which they are represented, conveys a hopeless sense of emptiness far more chilling than any more descriptive medium could evoke. What completes the horror of the sculpture is the casual way the museum visitor happens upon the scene, a room inhabited by anonymous effigies.

Address
Fifth Avenue at 82nd Street
New York, N.Y. 10028
✆ (212) 535 7710
Recorded information
(212) 879 5500

Map reference
㉓

How to get there
Subway: 4, 5, & 6.
Bus: M1, M2, M3, M4, M18,
& M79.

Opening times
Tue–Thur and Sun
9.30–5.15; Fri and Sat
9.30–9. Closed Mon, 25
Dec, 1 Jan, and
Thanksgiving.

Entrance Fee
By donation.

Tours
A wide range of tours and
gallery talks in most
languages.

The Metropolitan Museum was established as a national gallery and institute of art by a committee of New York citizens, for the most part members of the Union League Club. It was the President of the club, John Jay – the grandson of the first chief justice of the U.S. Supreme Court – who first suggested its foundation during a celebration dinner in Paris on the fourth of July. The museum was incorporated in April 1870, the responsibility being shared between the trustees and the city.

Originally the museum's holdings were housed at Dodsworth's Dancing Academy on Fifth Avenue, and then in the Douglas Mansion on West Fourteenth Street until the first permanent building opened in 1880 – a Neo-Gothic edifice designed by Calvert Vaux and Jacob Wrey Mould. The core of the collection was formed by acquisitions from the first director, General Louis Palma de Cesnola, of Cypriot antiquities and 170 paintings, for the most part Dutch and Flemish.

The central building, which originally faced south, was begun in the 1890s by Richard Morris Hunt and completed by his son Richard Howland Hunt in 1902. McKim, Mead and White added the north and south wings, with their entrances onto Fifth Avenue in 1911 and 1913, and the remaining wings – Lehmann, Sackler, American, Michael J. Rockefeller, and Lila Acheson Wallace – were all added by Kevin Roche John Dinkeloo between 1975 and 1987.

The pattern of acquisition at the Met has revealed its ambition to assemble a truly representative collection. The best from every period and part of the world can be found among its departments: Egyptian Art; Arms and Armour; European Sculpture and Decorative Arts; Medieval Art; Twentieth-century Art; Art of Africa the Americas and Pacific Islands; Greek and Roman Art; Asian Art; Musical Instruments; European Paintings; Islamic Art; Ancient Near Eastern Art; Drawings, Prints and Photographs; and the Costume Institute.

THE METROPOLITAN MUSEUM OF ART

More Roman than Egyptian, the Temple of Dendur was erected by the Emperor Augustus around 23–10 BC. at the end of his occupation of Egypt and Lower Nubia. The three parts of the building; pronaos, ante-chamber and sanctuary follow the traditional ceremonial plan for cult temples. In this case the temple was dedicated to the goddess Isis, but also to the two sons of a local Nubian chieftain who had drowned in the sacred River Nile. It is possible that one of the boys was buried in a tomb cut into the hillside behind the original site of the temple. The hieroglyphic reliefs depict Augustus shown as a pharoah making offerings, a curious and pragmatic example of colonial influence. In addition to these, years of tourist graffiti dating from the first century BC all the way through to the 1800s are inscribed in the stone.

The original site of the temple in Nubia was one of several destined to be submerged by the construction of the Aswan High Dam in 1960. It has recently been said that the presentation of the temple to the United States Government – in recognition of aid towards the restoration of Nubian monuments – was in great part facilitated by the influence of Jacqueline Kennedy Onassis. Following the construction of the Sackler Wing for its display the temple was installed at the Metropolitan in 1978.

Frescoes from Boscoreale

40–30 BC

The catastrophic eruption of Vesuvius in 62 BC decimated the thriving Roman communities of Boscoreale and Boscotrecase located in the environs of Pompeii, but also preserved important examples of domestic fresco paintings, of which the Metropolitan has a variety in its collection. From the villa of P. Fannius Synistor at Boscoreale five panels provide an insight into three of the lavish rooms; a central hall, an exedra and the entire bedroom, which allows a remarkably vivid idea of Roman mural painting and interior design. The wall panels show a naturalistic, almost *trompe l'oeil* views of land and townscapes. From Room 'H' of the villa, the largest room measuring twenty-five feet square, can be seen frescoes – originally framed by bossed Corinthian columns – which are thought to be recreations of lost Hellenic masterpieces depicting deities.

Head of a Bodhisattva, perhaps Siddhartha

2nd or 3rd century AD

This striking head has been identified as a personification of a Bodhisattva, or potential Buddha. Buddha was considered to have had several previous lives or stages of enlightenment characterized by his wise and divine qualities. Siddhartha was believed to be 'he who has accomplished his purpose', and is usually depicted as a young man of exceptional beauty. It is thought that it was in Gandhara, the cosmopolitan region of eastern Afghanistan, that the first artistic impressions of Bodhisattvas such as this one were made under Kushan rule; they were strongly influenced by the naturalism of Greco-Roman art. The present example derives much of its beauty from the clean, classical lines of the face modelled in warm terracotta. As was the case with many Greek and Roman sculptures, colour is introduced to the figure, here by means of the piercing garnet eyes.

Francesco d'Este

1460

Rogier van der Weyden

In 1444 Francesco d'Este, the illegitimate son of Lionello d'Este, Duke of Ferrara, was sent to Brussels as a military equerry and ambassador where he remained, in the service of the Burgundian dukes Philip the Good and Charles the Bold, until his death in the 1470s. At the time of this portrayal by the Flemish artist Rogier van der Weyden (1399/1400–1464) in 1460, Francesco was about thirty years of age. It is possible that the ring and hammer he holds in such a stylized manner refer to a recent victory at a tournament, although they have also been read as emblems of office. His heraldic authority is represented by the Este coat of arms painted on the reverse of the panel. The small scale and intimate framing of this portrait are mitigated by the aloof and distant attitude of the sitter, who holds clues to his identity but gazes resolutely out of the picture space.

The Harvesters

1565

Pieter Bruegel the Elder

This painting was one of a series of six scenes each representing two months of the year; the others are in the Kunsthistorisches Museum in Vienna. They were commissioned from Bruegel (c. 1525–69) by the Flemish financier Niclaes Jonghelinck. To the twentieth-century eye, the aerial view has become a convention of landscape and topography, whereas it was quite new to Bruegel's audiences. The dominance of landscape over subject matter was also innovatory, and here the artist makes all the details of the scene secondary to the evocation of late summer. None of the figures is accorded an individual identity apart from their role as field workers, and the colour and light effects specific to that warm and languid season serve to unite the vast sweep of nature into a harmonious whole.

The Adoration of the Magi

c. 1449

Andrea Mantegna

This early work by Mantegna (*c.* 1431–1506) is thought to have been painted while he was based at the Ferrarese court of the Este family in 1449. Mantegna's distinctive style of painting is already apparent here, although several of his influences can be discerned. From Jacopo Bellini, whose daughter he married, the artist derived a somewhat decorative approach to painting landscapes and natural formations such as the striated rocks and undulating river. Donatello, whose sculpture Mantegna first saw in Padua, has long been credited with inspiring his interest in psychological drama. The meticulous exactitude with which the scene is executed could be explained by the Estes' interest in Flemish painting, with which Mantegna was also familiar.

The focus of the painting is the Madonna who occupies a central position in the composition. She is shown in an attitude of veneration, praying to her infant son whom she has lain on the hem of her rich blue, red and gold cloak. Around the Virgin Mary and Christ Child hover seraphim and cherubim described in the same colours. To the left Joseph sleeps, seemingly removed from the sanctity of the moment. In contrast the two shepherds who have come to pay homage to the baby Jesus crane forward, one of them open-mouthed in amazement, only to show his toothless and shabby state. This remarkable play of the mundane and the sacred is continued up on the hillside where a tiny angel can be seen telling the shepherds in their pastures of the holy birth.

The sitter for this supremely elegant portrait by Bronzino (1503–72) has not been identified, but in all likelihood he was a Florentine aristocrat, as indicated by the *pietra serena*, the greenish-grey local stone of that city, and the grotesque Mannerist forms of the table and chair typical of Florence in that period. Equally Mannerist is the pose and countenance of the figure. One of the central tenets of that style was a quality known as *sprezzatura*, roughly translated as ease, grace, or stylishness for its own sake. The arrogant confidence with which Bronzino's subject stands, hand on hip, his sinuous fingers slotted into his book or splayed decoratively against his side, embodies the noble confidence central to court style of the mid-sixteenth century. The values and aesthetic of that society are memorably recorded in Baldassare Castiglione's *Book of the Courtier* where *sprezzatura* is advised and celebrated. Bronzino himself matches the assurance of the young man with his seamlessly perfect handling of the composition, paint and details of the sitter's costume. The intricate little flourishes of his tunic and hat, the slashing and the knotted sash around his waist are carried off as if they were the most natural or casual clothes. Furthermore, Bronzino restricts the range of colours to cold tones, with the result that even the nobleman's flesh appears as cool as his haughty demeanour.

Venus and the Lute Player

1560s

Titian (Tiziano Vecellio)

This is the last of the five paintings Titian (*c.* 1488–1576) executed on this theme. The subject is thought to relate to the Neo-Platonic debate as to whether the eye or the ear was the more suitable means for perceiving beauty. That the conundrum was the subject of a painting would have implicitly answered the question. Titian's interest in Neo-Platonism ran throughout the span of his almost sixty-year career as did his use of the reclining nude. He is thought to have first treated this theme when he was charged with completing his master Giorgione's *Sleeping Venus* of *c.* 1509, now in Dresden. In the Metropolitan painting Venus is shown to be as capable of participating in the art of music – and it is suggested, love – as the eager youth who sits by her, as demonstrated by the flute she idly holds and the guitar laid casually to one side. Perhaps the intended implication is that her mind is drawn to higher forms of love, given her abstracted gaze while Cupid crowns her with a garland of flowers.

Over the balustrade stretches an expanse of glimmering landscape, a remarkable example of Titian's late, painterly style. Patches of sunlight are rendered through the most immediate and gestural use of paint, and a surprising range of tones is picked up by the contrast between the warm golden tones of the valley and the ice-blue mountain peaks.

Rubens, his wife, Helena Fourment, and their Son Peter Paul

1635

Sir Peter Paul
Rubens

The portrait Rubens (1577–1600) painted of himself with his wife and son is set in the garden of his grandiose house and studio in the middle of Antwerp – the pavilion adorned with Classical caryatids can still be visited today. Now as then the house represented Rubens's revolutionary success as a painter and diplomat, both professionally and socially. Within five years of painting the picture he was knighted by Charles I. The very fact that he presents himself and his family in patrician terms, dressed in the most elegant court costume, bears witness to his achievement and pride.

Helena Fourment was Rubens's second wife whom he married after the death of Isabella Brandt when he was fifty-three and she was sixteen, and many of the portraits he did in this period celebrate the poetic ideals of the domestic idyll he had found with the much younger woman. This theme is appropriately known as The Garden of Love. In this case the pavilion is laced with roses and overgrown with vines, and a sense of exotic hedonism is emphasized by the parrot who seems to participate in the warm familial intimacy of the group. Several of the pictorial references are included as a celebration of fertility, such as the full-breasted caryatid, running fountain and rambling plants.

Portrait of Lucas van Uffele

1622

Sir Anthony van Dyck

Following his close apprenticeship with Rubens in whose workshop he achieved a precocious success, Van Dyck (1599–1641) followed the precedent of his master and travelled for several years through Italy in the early 1620s. In Venice he met Lucas van Uffele, a Flemish merchant and art collector whose portrait he painted twice. In this example, the more dynamic of the two versions, Van Uffele is shown in an active pose, glimpsed as he is about to rise and turn from his desk. The fingers of his right hand are splayed decorously against the arm of his chair, whereas in his other hand he holds a compass, as much for the elegant display of his fingers as any immediately discernable purpose, although all the objects shown refer to his accomplishments. As was a popular fashion with humanists in the fifteenth and sixteenth centuries, the table is covered with an oriental carpet on which are strewn a red-chalk drawing, celestial globe, antique bust, and recorder. By means of these lavish objects Van Uffele is celebrated as a connoisseur, scholar, musician and navigator, but most of all a gentleman. The depiction of an amateur shown surrounded by his artistic and scholarly possessions follows the tradition established by Titian's portrait of *Jacopo Strada* in the Kunsthistorisches Museum, Vienna and Lorenzo Lotto's *Andrea Odoni* in the Royal Collection, Windsor.

El Greco (Domenikos
Theotokopoulos)

El Greco's dramatic view of his adopted city is among the first paintings to have landscape as its primary subject. El Greco (1541–1614) was so called because he was born in Crete, where he trained as a painter of icons. In 1570 he went to Venice where he worked in Titian's studio before spending a short interval in Rome and departing for Spain in 1577. Titian's influence can be recognized in this painting, since it was he and his masters Giovanni Bellini and Giorgione before him who first imbued representations of landscape with significance, drama and sometimes nostalgia. In great part this was due to the light effects achieved through rich and expressive applications of oil paint to evoke specific atmospheric conditions or times of day.

Here El Greco has freely re-composed the town so that its more distinctive buildings are given prominence on the profile of the hill, and their outlines and architectural features are sharply illuminated by the weird, glowing light that often precedes a thunder storm. The sky itself forms patterns and gives dramatic emphasis to the painting with its range of black storm clouds (which conveniently hang behind the buildings to achieve a contrast) and explosive breaks in the clouds. The greater part of El Greco's mature work was imbued with a sense of religious intensity and mysticism, and in this case the magnitude of the weather and light effects in contrast to the tiny, ant-like men scrambling along the river does appear to comment on a recognition of a very definite cosmic order.

Young Woman with a Water Jug

Early 1660s

Jan Vermeer

New York is particularly rich in pictures by Vermeer (1632–75). Of the forty paintings convincingly attributed to him, three are in the Frick Collection, and three in the Metropolitan Museum. *Young Woman with a Water Jug* is an excellent example of Vermeer's studies of figures, usually women, at work on mundane activities. Here the protagonist is simply opening a window as she reaches for the water jug; whether the two activities are connected cannot be established. However, the study of the different qualities of light and its effect as it falls on the surfaces of the interior appears to be the foremost preoccupation. One of the most complex details of this picture is the description of the woman's hand holding the window frame. Through the patterned glass we can see her fingers highlighted by the sun. Vermeer's interest in light and texture is intricately explored by the reflections glimpsed in the brass jug and basin. The swathe of blue cloth that is draped over the chair appears again as an abstracted facet of blue, whereas the elaborate oriental rug covering the table is mirrored in the gleam of the metal. As in many of Vermeer's paintings, a map is included, neatly stretched on blue poles and hanging on the back wall of the room. This provides an incongruous reference to Dutch political power – in the 1660s the Netherlands were at the height of their naval hegemony – presented as a decorative domestic detail.

Commissioned by the Sicilian aristocrat Don Antonio Ruffo in 1653, this historicising portrait depicts Aristotle gazing meditatively on the statue of Homer. Through a drawn curtain can be seen a pile of books implying the literary and philosophical authority of Homer for Aristotle. In turn, Aristotle's own influence is indicated by the medallion he wears around his neck, depicting his pupil Alexander the Great in profile. The relationship between the three heroes of Greek antiquity is further complicated by the fact that Homer represents the dramatic and literary world, Aristotle the philosophical, and Alexander the political. The intimacy of the scene depends on the darkened room in which a concentrated beam of light picks out the sentimental reverie of Aristotle as he contemplates his mentor nostalgically.

Rembrandt (1606–69) was drawn to a somewhat theatrical depiction of historical subjects, and he is known to have owned props such as costumes, armour and Hellenic busts, of which the present example was one. Accordingly, Aristotle is shown dressed as a Renaissance humanist, from whom the Dutch first derived their interest in Classical scholarship. There is a possibility that Rembrandt was attempting his own version of the Renaissance conundrum as to whether painting or sculpture was the more naturalistic art form, the implicit answer being painting since here the bust, a sculpture, is rendered in paint.

The fame and prestige of the painting were enhanced by its purchase in 1961 for the unprecedented sum of $2.3 million.

Penitent Magdalene

1638–43

Georges de La Tour

Little is known about the career of Georges de La Tour (1593–1652) in the Duchy of Lorraine. His paintings range from rich, lavish scenes of worldly indulgence such as the *Card Sharps* or *The Fortune Teller,* shown in the same room of the Metropolitan, to spare and austere religious works. In the latter case it is likely that the artist was influenced by Counter-Reformation demands for clarity and immediacy in the depiction of sacred subjects. As with other representations of contrite and anguished saints shown isolated in the recognition of their sin, Mary Magdalene is set in an obscure and hermetically sealed room in which the only light source is a candle. Apart from infusing the place with a melancholic and poignant mood, the candle serves a symbolic purpose as a reference to the transitory nature of mortality. The fact that the candle is also reflected in the mirror further complicates its meaning, its significance is as passing as the reflection of the Magdalene's physical appearance. Her rejection of her former life as a prostitute and the material concerns of her past are indicated by the jewels she has cast to the floor. Similarly, we do not see her face full-on since the subject of the work is not her appearance, but her turning away from it in recognition of some inner truth.

Mezzetin

1718–20

Jean-Antoine Watteau

THE METROPOLITAN MUSEUM OF ART

The majority of paintings executed by Watteau (1684–1721) during his short career depicted scenes derived from the Commedia dell'Arte, a form of drama of Italian origin. In the early eighteenth century the plays and characters based on the Italian theatrical tradition of satire and farce had a widespread appeal in France. Initially staged at popular fairs and carnivals, the irreverent mockery of contemporary issues led to the Commedia actors being expelled in 1695. Until they regained legitimacy in 1714 the troupes operated underground while gaining an illicit popularity with the nobility and upper-middle classes. Watteau's depiction of Mezzetin, (whose name means 'half-measure'), the meddling confidential agent at the centre of most Commedia farces, shows him attempting a languid, melancholy, and ridiculous serenade. Watteau often used ornamental statuary as a form of chorus or comment on the goings-on of his hedonistic characters, so there is a possibility that the Classical sculpture turned resolutely away from Mezzetin's crooning may indicate the hopelessness of his attempts at seduction. The setting of this tragi-comic vignette in a grand Italianate park refers to the adoption of Commedia plays by upper-class amateurs.

Following Watteau's early death at the age of thirty-seven, *Mezzetin* was bought by his canny friend, the rich and enterprising Jean de Julienne, who spread the popularity and prestige of Watteau's work by commissioning prints after most of his paintings.

Boy Blowing Bubbles

1730s

Jean-Baptiste-Siméon Chardin

By the 1730s Chardin (1699–1779) had found widespread success at the Salon des Beaux-Arts with atmospheric but moralising genre scenes such as this little painting, one of several versions on the same theme. Here he pays tribute to the influence of Dutch *vanitas* pictures where a seemingly dispassionate and naturalistic rendition of everyday objects or occurences serves to remind the viewer of the fragility and transience of life. In this case the bubble could also signify feminine inconstancy and fickleness, a harsh reality that, it is suggested, this child and adolescent have yet to discover.

The youth of the two protagonists makes Chardin's scene all the more poignant. The nostalgia it is intended to suggest is made sharper by the fact that in their innocence the delicacy of the soap bubble means little save its immediate fascination. The artist establishes a telling contrast between the older boy, busy at his frivolous pastime, with the smaller child who cranes up as high as he can in order to see the bubble over the shelf. The intense stillness of Chardin's picture is achieved by his subtle, cool range of similar tones, and the gentle juxtaposition of different textures, the firm stone ledge and the weightless bubble.

EL S.D. MANUEL OSORIO MANRIQUE DE ZVÑIGA

The subject of this portrait was Don Manuel, the son of the Conde de Altamira, who was born in 1784. The count had commissioned Goya (1746–1828) to paint several members of his family in the period following the artist's appointment as court painter to the Bourbon King Charles III of Spain. Goya portrays the child as standing stiffly in a nondescript setting where the only sense of depth or specificity is established by the play of light and the animals that occupy the shallow background. The tones used to describe this setting are cool, modulated and recessive, against which the small boy's vivid red costume stands out distinctly. At the end of a loose draped string the child holds a magpie, which in turn carries Goya's professional calling card in its beak. More birds are held in a domed cage behind the boy, and from the shadowy left background of the painting two cats glare intently at the magpie. The child's face is portrayed as open and innocent, picked out by one of the two light sources of the composition. It has been suggested that the caged birds signify the boy's protected childhood, and the cats the dangers that await him beyond.

The Death of Socrates

1787

Jacques-Louis David

Although the subject of the death of Socrates – the great philosopher of Classical Athens – had been interpreted by several acclaimed artists in the eighteenth century, this depiction by David (1748–1825) met with an unprecedented reception at the Salon of 1787 and that of 1791 where it was shown after the height of the French Revolution. Much of the popularity and impact of the painting derived from moral and political parallels drawn between the repressive Athenian government, which had ordered Socrates to recant his criticism or be executed, and the abuses of the French Ancien Régime.

David's highly theatrical scene focuses on Socrates's decision to die at his own hand rather than renounce his beliefs. The cool, Neoclassical style used by David serves to invest his self-sacrifice with heroism. The grand old man is highlighted as he reaches absent-mindedly for the cup, so absorbed is he in his last insights and remarks. The public nature and importance of the suicide are glorified above private sentiment to the extent that Xanthippe, Socrates's wife, is seen small and cast in shadow as she and the family are ushered out before his death.

To ensure historical accuracy David consulted the scholar Abbé, and introduced details such as the lamp, cup and relief of the Athenian owl sculpted onto the side of the stone bench. A good deal of the pictorial authority of this large, frieze-like painting derives from formal quotations of the work of Poussin and Raphael.

The Island of the Dead
1880–1885
Arnold Böcklin

Arnold Böcklin (1827–1901) spent his career between Germany and Italy, where he painted the five versions of this image between 1880 and 1885. The version belonging to the Metropolitan is the first and was commissioned as a form of mourning painting by the recently widowed Marie Berna. Although the island has never been positively identified, it is reminiscent of San Michele, the cemetery island in the Venetian lagoon, and also of the Borromean islands in Lake Maggiore.

A romanticised form of Neoclassicism runs through Böcklin's work and in this mysterious and melancholic scene several motifs are drawn from ancient sources. In Egyptian and Greek mythology the idea of death was represented by a ferryman transporting the soul across water to its final resting place, and here the portent of that journey is enhanced by the spectre-like figures in the boat. Similarly, Böcklin draws on the classical tradition of depicting cypresses to locate a burial ground. The formal elements of the painting support the mood of the subject by means of a curious glowing light – a sinister illumination with no apparent source – and the dark sombre colours it picks up. The enigmatic quality of the painting greatly influenced the work of Giorgio de Chirico and qualified it as a seminal antecedent for the Surrealists.

The Young Ladies of the Village

1851–52

Gustave Courbet

Throughout his artistic career, Courbet (1819–77) was occupied with the challenge of depicting modern subject matter on a grand scale. Themes of social and pictorial reality, issues which previously would never have been seen suitable for paintings, were taken by Courbet and blown up onto the large canvases that were more usually destined for the academic Salon. In the case of *The Young Ladies of the Village*, Courbet relates an apparently trivial incident during a walk through the Communal, a valley in the region of his home town of Ornans. Courbet's three sisters, Zoë, Zélie and Juliette modelled for the genteel young women – clearly bourgeoise with their town clothes and refined manners – who stop to give money or food to a cowgirl. The yawning gap between the town and country is made clear by her puzzlement in respect to their assurance, her bare feet and their elaborate dress, her duties to the cows and their accompaniment by a jaunty but useless toy dog. Courbet had hoped to win his critics round with this work, the first of a series devoted to the lives of women, but they derided his efforts more than ever when it was exhibited at the Salon of 1852.

Boating

1874

Edouard Manet

Boating comes as close as any of Manet's works to Impressionism. Although he influenced and befriended several members of the Impressionist group, he never exhibited with them, and his paintings remain more concerned with significant human presences than the more objective, investigative pre-occupations of the Impressionist perspective. In this case Manet (1832–83) relegates most of his picture space to the two protagonists seen from close quarters at the end of a boat. Although the woman has never been definitively identified, the man was Manet's brother-in-law, Rodolphe Leenhoff. Monet – who had joined Manet for the summer at Argenteuil – painted many versions of the river in that area, and was concerned with the scenery under specific atmospheric effects. Manet, on the other hand, removed any question of specific topography by excluding the sky and river bank altogether. The focus of the painting, albeit under the conditions of summer leisure, is the man's acknowledgement of the spectator, and the suspense derived from the lack of immediate communication with his companion. This achieves a sense of both remoteness and intimacy; the spectator is party to this unconvivial couple through the adoption of a device taken from Japanese prints, the use of the frame to cut into the space of the subject. The study of sunlight falling on the man's shoulders, casting his tanned face into shadow, is one of the details of the painting that shows Manet influenced by Impressionist *plein air* painting.

Lady at a Tea Table

1885

Mary Cassatt

The subject of *Lady at a Tea Table* by Mary Cassatt (1844–1926) is her elder cousin, Mary Johnston Dickinson, who was married to Robert Moore Riddle. Although the portrait was greatly admired by Degas who considered it distinguished, the depiction of this steely old lady was badly received in the family, much to Cassatt's disappointment. For years it was stored away in a cupboard until Mrs. Havermeyer, Cassatt's childhood friend from Philadelphia and great patroness of the Metropolitan, encouraged her to exhibit it in 1914 and then donate it to the museum in 1923.

Mrs Riddle is portrayed as the epitome of domestic propriety, wielding the authority of the matriarch in charge of dispensing tea from a highly prized Canton china set. The colour scheme of the portrait is dominated by the blue and gold of the tea service which results in an expressive, if cold effect, by picking out the blue of the old lady's eyes. The several cups laid out on the table and Mrs. Riddle's gaze beyond the picture space imply that she is in company, but the intimate framing of the woman caught with an absent-minded expression of reverie also imbues the likeness with a sense of frank familiarity.

Woman with Chrysanthemums
1858–65
Edgar Degas

THE METROPOLITAN MUSEUM OF ART

Woman with Chrysanthemums was initially conceived as a still life of a bowl of flowers, influenced by similar still lifes executed by Delacroix. If it had remained as such it would have been a perfectly successful, somewhat exuberant, romantic study. With the addition of the woman who was painted in during 1865, Degas (1834–1917) extended the scene to encompass the formal and expressive concerns of his maturity. The sitter, positioned at the far left and all but cut off by the frame, is further marginalized by her gazing out of the picture space. This was a device which Degas and many of his contemporaries had adopted from Japanese prints. He continued to experiment with such casual placing which introduced an important aspect to modern painting – the question of what can be considered the subject of the picture if the figure does not occupy the focal space of the work. Also influenced by Japanese art, although less directly, was Degas's exploration of the complex play between surface pattern and form. From a very close range he juxtaposes the 'real' and three-dimensional flowers on top of the rich tablecloth against the flowered wallpaper behind. What rescues the 'real' flowers from being just another patterned surface is their full solidity and volume.

⭐ Madame Charpentier and her Children

1878

Pierre-Auguste Renoir

To the late twentieth-century eye Madame Charpentier may appear to be a perfectly conventional nineteenth-century figure in her long, high necked dress and glow of domestic order, but in its time this acclaimed portrait by Renoir (1841–1919) derived a great part of its success from its modernity. Madame Charpentier, shown wearing a highly fashionable Worth dress, is set against the latest vogue in interior design, Japanese wallpaper and furnishings. The composition is at once modern and conventional. The sitter occupies the centre of the picture space, forming an approximate but authoritative pyramid. However, the bold diagonal set by the pattern of the carpet and the way the dog is cut off by the frame, is drawn from Japanese prints. The poses of the little girls are consciously casual, due in great part to the patience of the dog. That Renoir was chosen to paint the family was a bold departure by the publisher Georges Charpentier and his wife, since the recognition he had received as an Impressionist painter was for landscapes rather than portraiture. The commission can be explained by the fact that the artist was part of the circle of intellectuals and artists that met on Friday evenings at the Charpentier's salon. Renoir's decision to submit this large and formal portrait to the Salon des Beaux-Arts rather than the Fourth Impressionist Exhibition was supported by Madame Charpentier.

Starting with Jacques Callot's depictions of court entertainments in the mid-seventeenth century, the subject of performance, be it popular or aristocratic, became a recurrent theme in French art. Seurat's relatively late painting concerns itself with a side show rather than the main event. What we and the row of silhouetted spectators shown from behind see is the parade for the Cirque Corvi, a show held on the pavement in the hope of luring the public into the performance. Of the very few paintings executed by Seurat (1859–91) this shows two of his recurring concerns: the spectacle of urban life, and that of performances such as the circus. Furthermore it displays the range of Seurat's technical and compositional interests. The paint is applied according to the principles of pointillism or divisionism whereby small dots of complementary colour jar or fuse with one another to create the intended tone. Moreover, the design of the painting follows theories proposed by the chemist Eugène Chevreuil, whereby lines leading upwards were thought to evoke happiness, with the opposite effect for lines leading downwards. Here examples of both types of line can be seen, in the frieze of gas lamps above the stage and in the stems of the musician's trumpets. The contradiction caused by the lines moving in different directions, as well as the colour scheme which is at once brilliant and sombre, could imply the artificial jollity of such popular entertainments.

The Card Players

1890s

Paul Cézanne

Cézanne (1839–1906) was one of a generation of Post-Impressionist painters concerned with the process of representation and expression as much the subject of the work itself. For the first time since the Renaissance, paintings ceased to be boxes mirroring the depth of the real world. Cézanne's approach is based on an awareness that a picture is at once an image and a pattern of paint and colour on a flat canvas.

After a period of study in Paris during the 1870s, Cézanne returned to Provence where he remained for the rest of his career, painting a small number of subjects in series, which allowed him to explore their formal characteristics in depth. In the case of the *Card Players*, Cézanne adopted a theme from a painting by Mathieu Le Nain in the museum at Aix-en-Provence, which depicts a rustic scene common to many local cafés, but also explores the arrangement of shape and tone traced by the players. Each figure forms an individual pyramid which is also part of a larger pyramid assembled round the table. The interaction between the men appears habitual but concentrated. They lean heavily on the table, demonstrating its solidity, but at the same time this illusion is challenged by the way Cézanne has rendered it with evident, faceted paint strokes. The flat wall behind the four men is as tangible and solid as any of the three-dimensional objects in the room.

THE METROPOLITAN MUSEUM OF ART

Quite apart from the consummate handling and colour of this painting, it is of central importance as the foremost Primitivist work of Gauguin's Tahitian period. Primitivism refers to the free borrowing from so-called primitive sources and styles used by modern artists of the Post-Impressionist school onwards. Although the context of Tahiti predominates in this complex masterwork (it accounts for the setting, the sitters and the title, which translates as 'I hail thee Mary'), there are two other important cultural quotations. First of all, that of Christianity – in the Madonna bearing Christ on her shoulder – with which Gauguin had already shown a fascination in his Pont Aven works. Secondly there is the more formal quotation of Polynesian art. Gauguin is known to have had in his possession a photograph of the Javanese temple at Borobodur, and the two central women shown in attitudes of devotion are depicted in the same pose as two of the figures from the temple's frieze.

One of Gauguin's recurring concerns was the representation of spiritual visions and apparitions. He believed that communities such as the Bretons had a simple approach to faith that enabled a clearer, visionary perception. The stylized and abstracted treatment of the scene implies that the procedings cannot be conventionally interpreted. The title's identification of this scene as a form of Annunciation is supported by the ethereal presence of the lightly painted Archangel Gabriel who floats into the scene from the left, masked by a white-flowered shrub.

Washington Crossing the Delaware

1851

Emanuel Gottlieb Leutze

A monumental painting that has become an icon of American culture, *Washington Crossing the Delaware* is a romanticized but academic painting which was executed by Leutze (1816–68) during a period spent in Düsseldorf. Although he researched the subject in depth there remain some historical inaccuracies, no doubt to allow for an image of greater dramatic impact. The scene follows the prescriptions for history painting established by the French and British academies of the eighteenth century, where a single incident is imbued with universal significance. The spectacle of the moment is anchored by the heroism of Washington's action. The decisive and determined crossing of a river as central to military and moral victory harks back to Roman history and Julius Caesar's auspicious journey across the Rubicon. While Leutze was working in Düsseldorf in 1848 he became the leader of a group of German revolutionaries plotting to overthrow Prussian domination. The American precedent of the 1776 War of Independence was seen as an encouraging model for contemporary revolutionary action. Leutze's painting was received with great acclaim in Germany, but when he took this, the second version, back to America in an attempt to sell it to Congress, a sale could not be agreed upon. Instead the image generated a considerable amount of money for him in a different way, from the sale of the many prints made after it.

The three sisters, daughters of the Hon. Percy Wyndham, sat for Sargent's portrait in the drawing room of their father's house at 44 Belgrave Square, London during the winter of 1899. From the left they are: Madeleine, who married Charles Adaire; Pamela, who married Edward Tennant, but later became Lady Glenconnor when he was ennobled; and Mary, who became Lady Elcho, later Countess of Wemyss. Part of that group of pre-World War One *jeunesse dorée* known as The Souls, they are depicted in the glory of their femininity, overlooked by the portrait of their mother by G. F. Watts. The image of three women grouped in a formal arrangement which roughly corresponds to two profiles and one full-face, as well as the obvious celebration of youth and beauty, indicates Sargent's adoption of the Classical theme of the Three Graces.

The central composition of the sisters grouped around a silk damask-covered sofa plays on the many tones of white that constitute their skin and clothes. With such a narrow range of colour, Sargent was able to lavish the most sensuous and painterly attention on the many luxurious textures found adorning the women and their surroundings.

This magnificent group portrait was greatly acclaimed and continued to impress the art world when it was sold to the Metropolitan for £20,000 in 1925. On the eve of World War Two it was further celebrated by Cecil Beaton's photograph, closely based on this painting, of the Wyndham Quinn Sisters.

Room from the Francis W. Little House

1912–14

Frank Lloyd Wright

Although Frank Lloyd Wright (1867–1959) trained with one of the seminal architects of the skyscraper, Louis Sullivan, his work was predominantly suburban or rural. New York can offer one of his most important public buildings for the city in the form of the Solomon R. Guggenheim Museum, but this room from the Francis W. Little House – bought by the Metropolitan when the house was torn down in 1972 – provides an excellent example of his architecture and interior design for country houses. The house was originally set in a wood by Lake Minnetonka in Wayzata, Minnesota, and this room was where the Littles entertained and held concerts often performed by Mrs. Little, who was a musician.

Central to Wright's vision was the notion of 'organic space' as applied to domestic or public architecture, and here the striking length of the room is balanced by the flanking windows that run down its side. As with many of his commissions, Wright was responsible for designing the structure of the building, its decoration and furnishings. He ensured that the intimacy of the room was not lost by tying its many parts together with repeating motifs such as the rectangular panels picked out in light wood on the ceiling, windows and design of the furniture. Like many artists of his generation, Wright was deeply influenced by Japanese style, seen here in the free-flowing space of a room unencumbered by partitions, but also in smaller details such as the lamps and prints.

Gertrude Stein and her brother Leo were expatriate Americans, part of the circle of intellectuals and artists living in Paris who first supported and celebrated the work of Picasso (1881–1973) and Matisse. Although a work of great intensity, the portrait is painted in a transitional style of Picasso's career. He began working on it during the winter of 1905, but stopped when, as he said, 'I can't see you any longer when I look…' The sittings resumed after the autumn of 1906 following an important visit to Spain when Picasso became influenced by Iberian sculpture. The linear treatment of the face has the mask-like quality of Iberian figures, and although it was first thought that the sitter did not resemble the portrait, Picasso gave the ominous assurance 'She will.' Indeed, Stein thought it the best likeness of her ever done. The photographs that remain of Gertrude Stein up until her death in 1946 do show a close similarity, and as with any effective portrayal this also extends to her bearing and the hunched, somewhat monolithic quality of her body. The reduction of Stein's face to an arrangement of interlocking planes can be seen as the roots of the Cubist style where three-dimensional form is analyzed by means of its reduction to facets, or planes. Another aspect of the portrait which distinguishes it from preceding paintings of Picasso's Blue and Rose Periods is his colour range based on monochromes which do not detract from the formal investigation of the painting.

Autumn Rhythm (Number 30)

1950

Jackson Pollock

Jackson Pollock (1912–56) was a central figure in the group of artists who were first active at the end of the 1930s which came to be known as The New York School, or more widely Abstract Expressionists. This large-scale and portentous canvas has some grounding in representation, as can be seen in the rich autumnal colour range, but the main theme underlying the work of Pollock and his contemporaries was the use of paint and gesture as an expressive medium. Pollock and his wife Lee Krasner were most pre-occupied with what has come to be known as drip painting, a description which does nothing to convey the full impact of the technique. Fortunately Pollock is recorded on film while painting, or rather dancing around the canvas which would be pinned to the ground. This approach more than any other part of Pollock's work reveals his fundamental debt to the Surrealists, particularly those artists concerned with chance. The sequence of paint layers would be very carefully considered, and indeed the individual tension of the component colours does remain strong, each holding its own part in the composition despite the haphazard quality of the process and result. For instance Pollock never lost sight of the overall tension of the work, and the margins of the canvas serve as a form of secondary framing which contains the central dynamism of the composition. Consequently pictures such as *Autumn Rhythm* maintain an intriguing balance between chaos and the carefully choreographed, internally structured result.

Built 1765

The Morris-Jumel Mansion allows a rare and fascinating glimpse into Colonial life in New York. Although Harlem has now grown up around the house, its position on a hill overlooking the East River gives an idea of the rural splendour of the northern tip of Manhattan before the Revolution. The interiors are arranged to trace the early history of the house through its furnishings which range from the provincial to the cosmopolitan.

The mansion, a summer villa, was built in 1765 by Colonel Roger Morris and his wife Mary Philipse. Morris, a prominent Tory, returned to England when the Revolution broke out, leaving the house to be occupied by Washington as a strategic headquarters. Subsequently the mansion was used as a tavern until it was bought in 1810 by Stephen Jumel, a French merchant of great wealth who married the racy Eliza Bowen. After spending the years between 1815 and 1826 in France, Madame Jumel refurbished the house in fashionable Empire style. When Jumel died in 1832, Eliza did not hesitate long to get remarried, to former Vice-President Aaron Burr.

Address
65 Jumel Terrace between W 160th and 162nd Street
New York, N.Y.
✆ 212 923 8008

Map reference

How to get there
Subway: 1B during the week; C at weekends.
Bus: M2, M3, 18, 101.

Opening times
Wed to Sun 10–4.
Closed Mon, Tue.

Entrance fee
$3 adults, $2 senior citizens and students. Children under 10 free when accompanied by an adult.

Address
2 Lincoln Square
Columbus Avenue and 66th
Street
New York, N.Y. 10023
✆ 212 977 7298

Map reference

How to get there
Subway: 1, 2, 3, 9, A, B, C,
and D.
Bus: M5, M7, M10, M30,
M66, and M104.

Opening times
Tue to Sun, 11.30–7.30.
Closed Mon.

Entrance fee
Free.

Tours
Group tours by arrangement
✆ 212 595 9533.

The Museum of American Folk Art was established in 1961 to exhibit folk art ranging from the eighteenth century to the present. The collection comprises objects of a great variety of purpose from paintings and sculptures to furniture, textiles, carved animals and decoys. However, the very nature of folk art, which rarely follows any form of official or public programme and can include unique and whimsical examples, defies generalized categories. It provides much of the pleasure derived from extraordinary combinations of function, motif, technique and decoration. For instance, among the better known exhibits in the museum are a gate, dating from the nineteenth century and made from painted wood, which represents a somewhat inexact American flag. Also popular is a nine-foot copper weather vane, also from the nineteenth century, showing an Indian who has come to be known as St. Tammany. In this way, the museum provides a fascinating insight into some obscure aspects of American history. The references are familiar, but the exact context of their production is tantalizingly curious. The face and iconic authority of George Washington are ubiquitous to any native or traveller in the United States, if for no other reason than that of Gilbert Stuart's portrait printed on every one dollar bill. But there remains no evidence of the identity of the author of an equestrian portrait of the first President except that he was working in southeastern Pennsylvania around 1810.

While a permanent home for the Museum of American Folk Art is being constructed, the collection and important exhibitions are being shown at Lincoln Square. After the new building is completed the Lincoln Square site will serve as a branch museum. The new space will be larger and allow a permanent display of its significant holdings as well as major thematic exhibitions.

Girl in a Red Dress with Cat and Dog
1834–36
Ammi Phillips

For many years Ammi Phillips' oeuvre was divided among three recognized identities, that of Phillips, that of the 'Border Limner' active between 1811 and 1820, and that of the 'Kent Limner' active between 1830 and 1840. Recent scholarship has confirmed that all three were Phillips (1788–1865), a self-taught painter whose subjects – farmers, town professionals, and landowners – lived in Connecticut and along the Hudson River. The social position of an artist such as Phillips was somewhat ambiguous as seen in this letter from a contemporary, John Vanderlyn, to his nephew: 'Were I to begin life over again, I should not hesitate to follow this path, that is, paint portraits cheap and slight, for the mass of folks can't judge of the merits of a well-finished picture... Moving about the country as Phillips did and probably still does must be an agreeable way of passing one's time... gain more money than you could by any mechanical business, which you must know is far more laborious and less genteel and considered'

Nowadays, however, *Girl in a Red Dress with Cat and Dog*, a harmonious and sympathetic likeness of a child and her pets, is considered one of the masterworks of the Museum of Folk Art.

Address
Fifth Avenue at 103rd Street
New York, N.Y. 10029
 212 534 1672

Map reference
㉖

How to get there
Subway: 6
Bus: M1, M3, and M4.

Opening times
Wed to Sat 10–5. Tue 10–2
for pre-registered groups
only. Sun and legal holidays
1–5. Closed Mon.

Entrance fee
Free.

Tours
By arrangement with the
Education Department.

The Museum of the City of New York was the first institution of its kind to focus on the history of a city. Before the existing purpose-built premises were inaugurated in 1932, the museum was housed at Gracie Mansion, the summer villa built for merchant Archibald Gracie in 1799, and latterly the residence of the Mayor of New York. Money for the establishment and construction of the museum were raised by popular subscription.

Essentially a didactic, historical museum, the collections range from very fine examples of fine and decorative arts to ephemera such as toys and graphic material. The ITT Gallery on the ground floor helps to organize the collection into context by means of a multimedia presentation. Through an exhibition of dioramas, models and tiles, the Dutch Gallery attempts to reconstruct a sense of the city in its early incarnation as New Amsterdam. On the first floor can be found a sequence of period rooms, a gallery dedicated to marine paintings and nautical objects, and three collections belonging to Alexander Hamilton, the first secretary of the U.S. Treasury; Mrs Giles Whiting, a connoisseur of Federal decorative arts and furniture; and J. Clarence Davies. The last gallery includes Winslow Homer's *Union Pond, Williamsburg, Long Island* and Francis Guy's *View of Brooklyn*.

The General Mills Toy Gallery on the second floor contains dolls and dolls' houses including The Stettheimer House made in 1925 by Carrie Stettheimer. Her parents were friends with contemporary artists Marcel Duchamp, Alexander Archipenko, William Zorach and Gaston Lachaise, who helped to furnish the house with doll-size paintings and sculptures. Also on this floor is a revolving exhibition of portraits, *New York Faces 1820–1920*. Full-size period rooms, from the early nineteenth-century Bekard House and from the lavish 1860s Rockefeller House can be seen on the second and fourth floors.

The initial impetus to establish The Museum of Modern Art, or MoMA as it is widely known, came from three influential collectors of modern art: Abby Aldrich Rockefeller, Lillie Bliss, and Mrs. Cornelius J. Sullivan. In 1929 the museum was inaugurated, by director Alfred H. Barr Jr., with an exhibition of works by Cézanne, Gauguin, Seurat and Van Gogh. Barr's two ground-breaking exhibitions of the 1930s were 'Cubism and Abstract Art' and 'Fantastic Art, Dada, and Surrrealism'. The catalogues accompanying those shows remain, to this day, seminal works on twentieth-century art. A recognition that modernism was a multidisciplinary field motivated the establishment of the Departments of Architecture and Design in 1932, Photography in 1940, and Film in 1935.

The present building was constructed on the site of a Rockefeller family house by Edward Durrel Stone and Philip L. Goodwin in 1939. Philip Johnson designed the East Wing in 1964, and the most recent addition of the West Wing was built by the firm of Cesar Pelli and Associates with Gruen Associates in 1984. Above the West Wing is a residential block, Museum Tower, which helps to generate money for the museum.

The Museum of Modern Art owns a remarkably comprehensive survey of modern art, liberally sprinkled with some of the most innovatory and beautiful works of the century. The collection encompasses a rich and representative group of sculptures, some of which are shown in the galleries, and some in the Abby Aldrich Rockefeller Sculpture Garden which was formed after the 1860s Rockefeller house which had previously occupied that site was torn down in 1938. The museum's preoccupation with a multidisciplinary approach to modern and contemporary art has recently been elaborated by exciting and somewhat iconoclastic exhibitions such as those addressing the impact of Primitivism (1984), and the once-in-a-lifetime exhibition *Henri Matisse: A Retrospective* (1992).

Address
11 West 53rd Street
New York, N.Y. 10019
✆ 212 708 9480

Map reference

How to get there
Subway: E and F
Bus: M1, M2, M3, M4, and M5

Opening times
Sat to Tue, 11–6 .Thur and Fri 12–8:30. Closed Wed, Thanksgiving and Christmas.

Entrance fee
$8 adults, $5 students and senior citizens. Children under 16 accompanied by an adult free. Voluntary contributions on Thur between 5 and 8:30.

Tours
Daily tours, lectures, and films.

Château Noir

1904–06

Paul Cézanne

The highly sensuous but analytical paintings of Cézanne (1839–1906) tend to focus on a limited number of motifs found in the environs of Aix-en-Provence where he worked for most of his life. The Château Noir was one of these, and in this late landscape painted just before his death in 1906, the subject is represented in the artist's most mature style. The aspect he has taken allows him to divide the picture plane into three distinct diagonal areas from the lower left-hand corner up: the deep, impenetrable scrub; the ordered structure of the building; and the infinite sky beyond. Although each area can be read as such, Cézanne also used the same faceted brush stroke to describe each part, so that sky and building are endowed with a formal equivalence which questions the illusionism of the painting. We are at once transported to the hazy, vibrant landscape of Provence while being reminded of the underlying, painted structure of the image. That the painting does not lose its evocative power through analysis is explained by a rather humble letter Cézanne wrote to his son in 1906: 'I must tell you that as a painter I am becoming more clear-sighted before Nature, but with me the realization of my sensations is always painful. I cannot attain the intensity that is unfolded before my senses. I do not have the magnificent richness of colouring that animates nature.'

From early in the painting's history *Les Demoiselles d'Avignon* was hailed as an important work. One of the most immediate reactions to its classical brutality was that of Picasso's close collaborator Braque, who said that it made him feel as though he had been 'drinking turpentine and breathing fire'. But it would seem that Picasso (1881–1973) too was aware of the portent of this image, a considerably larger painting than the Blue Period works that preceded it, or the Cubist studies that it engendered. The size of the painting and its references to academic traditions makes it a far more public proclamation than the small, investigative canvases that followed it. At first the subject was to be a modern *vanitas* painting showing a sailor inspecting a parade of prostitutes at a brothel, the morbid consequences of his choice indicated by a bowl of decomposing fruit placed in the foreground. Studies for *Les Demoiselles* show the gradual disappearance of the sailor, only to be replaced, it is implied, by the viewer of the painting. The painting shows the two important 'Primitive' influences behind Picasso's development of Cubism: Iberian sculpture, seen in the linear treatment of the heads, and African masks, apparent in the severe, striated quality of the faces. From Cézanne, Picasso adopted a concern for the problems of representing three-dimensional reality on a flat plane – the starting point for Cubism. Thus the formal concerns of this painting support the subject. The central figure seen squatting, her legs splayed, is at once being 'shown' from several angles by Picasso, and showing herself to her prospective client.

The City Rises

1913

Umberto Boccioni

Boccioni (1882–1916) was the most prominent of five painters who chose to follow the example of Filippo Tommaso Marinetti and declare themselves Futurists. Marinetti's *Futurist Manifesto* of 1909 had proclaimed war against tradition and history in favour of a violent and energetic celebration of modernity as seen in many forms from war to speed. By the following year the *Technical Manifesto of Futurist Painting* was launched, in which it was announced: 'We sing of great crowds excited by work, by pleasure, and by riot; we will sing of the multicoloured, polyphonic tides of revolution in the modern capital.' The energetic vortex of men and workhorses in Boccioni's *The City Rises* certainly follows Futurist prescriptions. The spectator, as they had promised, is placed 'in the centre of the picture'. But it was to be some months before they adopted more modern techniques of painting based on the fragmented forms of Cubism. Here Boccioni still depends on painting with sharp divisionist brush strokes, a style more used in the 1880s than at the vanguard of twentieth-century avant-garde art. The development of Futurism can be clearly traced through the excellent collection in MoMA. Boccioni is particularly well represented since the museum also owns a cast of his revolutionary, if somewhat robotic bronze sculpture *Unique Forms of Continuity in Space.*

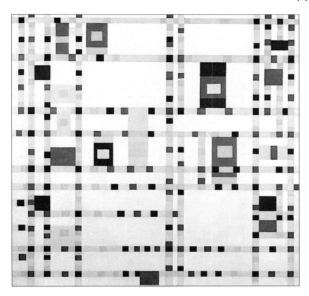

Some of the spare and rectilinear paintings created by Mondrian (1872–1944) defy any relationship to concrete subject matter beyond the arcane Theosophical ideas he believed in. Theosophy, 'the hidden religion' to which Kandinsky also adhered, proposed that beyond the material world lay a cosmos of significance and spirituality. The grids of Mondrian's paintings have consequently been interpreted as celebrating harmonious mathematical relationships between sky and earth – 'equilibrated relationships' as Mondrian described them. This approach becomes a little less vague when one looks at early works such as the two that hang in the same room of the Museum of Modern Art as *Broadway Boogie Woogie*: *Dunes and Sea* of 1909–10, and *Pier and Ocean* of 1914. However, *Broadway Boogie Woogie*, Mondrian's last completed work, is a painting which evokes several aspects of New York at once. Mondrian's style was well suited to a rendering of the street grid of the city, but here the usually rigorous transection of the canvas by line has been interrupted by small blocks or facets which recall the shuttling of the traffic, the regular switching of the lights, but also, as supported by the title, the syncopated rhythms of American jazz. Mondrian achieved recognition late in his life and *Broadway Boogie Woogie* was one of the paintings to feature in the first one-man show held for him in New York in 1942.

Bird in Space

1928

Constantin
Brancusi

Bird in Space is the final distillation of a theme which preoccupied the Rumanian sculptor Brancusi (1876–1957) for much of his career: the motif of the bird as a spirit of flight. By the time he created this work the recurrent bird motif had undergone a process of refinement and abstraction that resulted in pure form, highly dependent on the materials in which it was rendered. Brancusi was predominantly a carver, but as was the case here, when he had arrived at the core of his idea, he would be led to experiment with the effect of other materials. This unique cast in bronze enhances a sense of soaring flight by means of the highly polished surface and gleaming metal. As was often the case, Brancusi juxtaposes two contrasting materials, thus enhancing the reflective properties of the sculpture with the heavy graininess of the cylindrical marble base below. But beyond this reliance on materials there remains a unitary quality to Brancusi's sculptures in which there are rarely seen elements which detract from the fundamental core of the form, a concern he always returned to in his work, of which he said: 'What is real is not the external form, but the essence of things.'

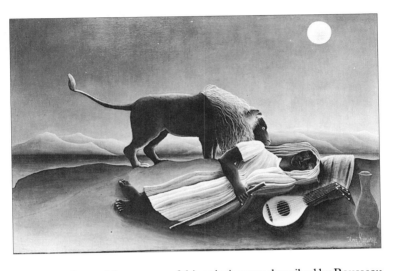

The mysterious subject matter of this painting was described by Rousseau (1844–1910) in a letter to the Mayor of Laval dating from 1898, in which he offered the work which he described as 'a genre painting' for sale at 1800 to 2000 francs. His letter told of a negress wandering through the desert who had stopped to drink from her jar, but being tired, had fallen asleep with her mandolin laid beside her. A lion approaches, but rather than devouring her, gently sniffs at her hair as she sleeps. The inconsequential, but languid quality of the painting caused it to be acclaimed by the Surrealists who first brought it to public attention in 1923. It seemed an ideal illustration of their celebration of the poetic results derived from inexplicable or chance encounters. Indeed, it was considered so perfectly bizarre and lacking in conventional subject matter that many presumed it to have been a forgery by André Derain, until the letter to Laval became known, and the authenticity of the painting was definitively established.

The content of the painting seems to have no significance other than the immediate episode set in a gleaming and tropical moonlight, but with Rousseau's grand scale (the canvas measures 2.60 by 1.90 metres) and the use of such classical devices as the central placement of the lion and the reclining nude, *The Sleeping Gypsy* takes on an incongruous and naive magnificence.

Dance

1909

Henri Matisse

This elegant and pleasurable painting by Matisse (1869–1954) is important in its own right, but also because it influenced the Russian collector Sergei Schukin to commission another version (*Dance II*) together with *Music* for his house in St. Petersburg. After seeing the Museum of Modern Art's painting he wrote to the artist: 'I find your panel *Dance* of such nobility that I am resolved to brave our bourgeois opinion and hang on my staircase a subject with nudes.'

Matisse's painting is typically concerned with a scene of pure pleasure and hedonism, and it is said that he was influenced by seeing fishermen dancing the 'sardana' on the beach at Collioure in southwest France in 1905. The unity of the group and harmonious simplicity of their movements relies to a great extent on the reduced colour scheme where just three tones are used, for expression rather than representation as Matisse explained: 'When I put down a green, that doesn't signify grass; when I put down a blue, that doesn't mean sky… All my colours sing together, like a chord in music.' The audacious design he adopted also serves to compliment the movement of the dancers; the centre of the composition is but a void around which the figures circle at the margins of the picture space.

Meret Oppenheim (1913–85) was a German-Swiss painter and sculptor working on the margins of the Surrealist group. She exhibited this *Object*, otherwise known as *Luncheon in Fur* at the Exhibition of Surrealist Objects held in Charles Ratton's House in Paris, in 1936. The marriage or 'chance encounter' of an object as mundane and functional as a cup and saucer with an organic and sensuous covering of fur qualified the sculpture as the ultimate in Surrealist irrationality. What makes the piece all the more effective is the way the nap of the fur is arranged to complement the structure of cup, saucer and spoon. Much of the disruptive effect of the *Object* derives from the comforting associations of both warm drinks and the luxury of fur, which when combined are disconcerting and unsettling. For precisely these reasons, it was highly acclaimed by the 'Pope' (as Dali dubbed him) of the Surrealist group, André Breton, who was motivated by it to write his seminal article *Crisis of the Object*, published in the May edition of *Cahiers d'art* of that year, in which he promoted 'the fabrication and circulation of objects appearing in dreams.'

Person Throwing a Stone at a Bird

1926

Joan Miró

MUSEUM OF MODERN ART

Although André Breton, the leader of the Surrealists proclaimed Joan Miró (1893–1983) as 'the most Surrealist of us all', this Catalonian painter's relationship to the Surrealist group was somewhat marginalized by his determined anti-intellectualism. However, his style of painting and child-like formal vocabulary as seen in *Person throwing a Stone at a Bird* is fundamentally indebted to the Surrealist technique of automatism or automatic writing. As described in Breton's seminal definition of Surrealism, pure 'psychic automatism' was the most direct means to 'the actual functioning of thought'. Miró appeared to corroborate this in 1933 by explaining that his painting was 'always born in a state of hallucination due to a shock of some kind – subjective or objective – for which I bear no responsibility'. More than in many of Miró's works, it is possible to trace the narrative implied in the title of the painting; the large white biomorph appears to be rocking back on his only heel as the stone travels towards the bird. The stone's trajectory seems to be implied by the thin black line transecting the person and indicating the stone as it hurtles towards the agitated bird below.

The Persistence of Memory

1931

Salvador Dali

Whereas some Surrealist painters attempted to reach the inner irrational workings of the mind by means of 'pure psychic automatism', a rapid and uninhibited marking of the canvas, Dali's technique was far more deliberate. The detailed accuracy of scenes such as this was intended to draw on the absurdity of dream imagery and corresponds to a description offered by Dali himself of his work as 'hand-painted photographs'.

Dali (1904–89) was a tireless self-publicist who conceived his own terminology to further complicate possible interpretations of his work. 'Be persuaded' he assured, writing in the third person, 'that Salvador Dali's famous limp watches are nothing else than the tender, extravagant and arbitrary paranoiac-critical camembert of space and time.' Bizarre juxtapositions such as the detail of the ants devouring a gold watch, or the oozing substance that takes on a human face he explained, or rather mystified, as the effect of his 'paranoiac-critical method' where one thing can have two possible interpretations, or what is expected of reality can be subverted. The soft watches are intended to disturb on two levels; not only have the objects themselves undergone some mysterious alteration, but by implication the whole dimension of time has no effect in Dali's unnervingly accurate landscape.

Grandmother

1925

Arthur Dove

The majority of Dove's work is made up of paintings of natural subjects rendered in a Cubist, but very lyrical, almost sonorous style. However, during the 1920s when Dove (1880–1946) took off with his family to live on a boat, he started working with collages. In *Grandmother* the image is assembled through references to an archetypal ideal of a reverend old lady in a softly faded and dilapidated style. The foundation of the picture is made up of sun-bleached panels of wood over which has been hung a fragment of embroidered cloth with a flowered pattern. Where the needle-point frays away is placed an equally disintegrating page from the *Concordance* on which are strewn brown and withered pressed flowers. The poignancy of the image relies as much on the nostalgic references of the elements as the questions they raise about age and decay.

Visa

1953

Stuart Davis

Visa is a painting typical of Davis' mature style and as such is an important antecedent to the commercial imagery of Pop Art. Although Davis (1894–1964) trained under artists of the Ash Can School and then went on to work in several idioms indebted to Van Gogh, Cézanne and the Cubists, by the 1950s his work had settled with exuberant images celebrating the city on a most mundane and ephemeral level. Central to this was Davis's use of lettering: 'I often use words in my pictures, because they are part of urban subject matter,' he said in 1950. In the case of *Visa* the central motif 'Champion' refers to a matchbook cover, but the inclusion of the phrase 'The amazing continuity' serves to enhance the composition by 'animating the area at the extreme right.'

MUSEUM OF MODERN ART

Wyeth (born 1917) has been associated with the American Regionalist school of painting: a group of artists who rejected European Modernism in favour of an exact and evocative style concerned with mundane or familiar aspects of American life. *Christina's World* is Wyeth's most reproduced work, the subject of which he clarified in the following explanation: 'Her physical limitations are appalling. The challenge to me was to do justice to her extraordinary conquest of a life which most people would consider hopeless. Christina's world is outwardly limited – but in this painting I tried to convey how unlimited it really is.'

The subject was Wyeth's neighbour who had been crippled by polio. She is identified here more by her disability than her identity since she is painted in a twisted pose seen from the back. Wyeth intended to show her picking berries, but this is not readily obvious and much of the underlying tension of the painting comes from the composition. The placement of the horizon high up on the picture plane increases a sense of desolation. The houses appear very distant in relation to the expanse of field, and implicit in the narrative of the scene is the woman's arduous crawl across the meadow.

I and the Village

1911

Marc Chagall

Before settling in Paris between 1910 and 1914, Chagall (1889–1985) had trained in St. Petersburg under Leon Bakst in his experimental school of theatre design. At that stage he was working in a Symbolist style. However, once he arrived in Paris his painting shifted to take on the brilliantly coloured and dynamic Cubist or 'Orphic' style of Robert Delaunay, as can be seen in *I and the Village*. In this picture Chagall assembles a nostalgic composition of life in his native village of Vitebsk. The two larger figures who face each other in a meaningful but speechless dialogue are a man and his cow. Against their respectful exchange are shown vignettes of rural life rendered in a fantastical and naive style. A reaper's walk up the village street is suddenly disrupted by his companion's inversion, accompanied by that of two of the houses.

Amongst the urban sophisticates of Paris the painting gained the highest praise. The poet Guillaume Apollinaire visited Chagall's studio and proclaimed it 'Supernatural!' whereas André Breton later pronounced: 'His full, lyrical eruption dates from 1911. It was then, in his work alone, that metaphor made its triumphal entry into modern painting.' In contrast Chagall's view of his pictures was far less portentous: 'I don't understand them at all. They are not literature. They are only pictorial arrangements of images that obsess me…'

Diary of a Seducer

1945

Arshile Gorky

In 1920 Gorky (1905–48) arrived in America from Armenia at the age of fifteen, and from 1925 for the subsequent twenty years or so his paintings developed towards his mature style, an idiom dependent on both Cubism and Surrealism, but a successful and original synthesis of both. From Surrealism Gorky derived an inventive method of drawing in front of nature whereby he would transcribe what he saw in the form of free, imaginative doodles to be translated into paint back at the studio. His debt to Surrealism was acknowledged, and to some extent appropriated by André Breton as can be seen in his homage to Gorky: '…Gorky is of all the Surrealists, the only one who maintains a direct contact with Nature and sits down in front of her to paint. Nature for him is not an *end* however; he seeks in Nature such sensations as will serve him as a springboard towards the deeper exploration of certain states of being.' From a matrix of thin paint, richly coloured, emerge biomorphic shapes that imply some form of life and expression, carefully drawn from the surrounding background. In the case of *Diary of a Seducer* the natural references which Breton dubbed 'hybrid' are combined with formal quotations from the most revered Old Masters. Elaine De Kooning, who was the second wife of the painter, identified Jacques-Louis David's *Mars Disarmed by Venus* of 1824 as a formal source. Gorky was known to have had an issue of *Dance Index* illustrating the painting on its cover.

Dog

1952

Francis Bacon

For the most part, paintings by Bacon (1910–92) are figurative, representing men isolated in hermetic and anonymous contexts. The Museum of Modern Art's painting of a dog is one of few pictures he executed of animals, but it shares with the human subjects of his repertoire a sense of desolation and anguish. The settings of Bacon's work are bare, stage-set like spaces in which the protagonists are caught in movements which can range from love-making to the most subtle shifts in pose. This Bacon achieves through a masterly but free use of oil paint. In the case of the dog there is some indication that it has been caught as it passes diagonally across the 'stage' of the canvas, given the tracks it has left as it goes, but at the same time with its white coat and desperate, exhausted stance it firmly occupies the middle ground. Bacon, whose roguish charm is well documented in spoken and filmed interviews, consistently refused to clarify his work, but the paintings trace conflicting but poetic concerns central to man's existence. A theme of hopeless isolation runs through every image, while at the same time their grand scale celebrates the inherent beauty of the most inconsequential moments.

Gold Marilyn

1962

Andy Warhol

Warhol (1930–87), the foremost exponent of Pop Art, was particularly concerned with the iconic power of popular heroes such as Marilyn Monroe, Jackie Kennedy and Elvis Presley. Their appearance transformed into pictorial motifs implied much more than their own identities; it suggested the idolatry they inspired and the mass consumerism they could generate. Although in this example Warhol has isolated Monroe's face against a gold background to imply an art historical pun on the theme of the Byzantine icon, many of his related silkscreens show the face repeated up to a hundred times. The play on a pseudo-religious veneration of the subject is conscious given the tongue-in-cheek quality of Warhol's titles such as *Marilyn Monroe Diptych*, in the Tate Gallery, London.

Zig VII

1964

David Smith

David Smith (1908–65) was originally from Indiana, where he worked as a steel worker in a car factory, and on the construction of locomotives. In 1926 he moved to New York where he began painting, but eventually shifted to sculpture as his work took on greater relief and became more three-dimensional. At this stage he was also considerably influenced by the metal constructions of Picasso and Julio Gonzalez. Smith's work divides into thematic and stylistic groups of which the Zigs are some of the most important. Like the brightly coloured, rhythmic *Zig VII*, they have a painterly quality which has led critics to align them with the 'Hard Edge' school of the Abstract Expressionists.

SAINT PETER'S AT CITICORP

Built 1977

Address
619 Lexington Avenue, at
54th Street
New York

Map reference
(28)

How to get there
Subway: 4, 5, 6, E, F.
Bus: M101, M102.

Opening times
Open for meditation during
the day.

Entrance fee
Free.

Saint Peter's Lutheran Church at the Citicorp
Center is a humane and pragmatic inclusion of
a religious space in what is otherwise a relent-
lessly corporate, commercial monolith. At the
base of the characteristically slanted tower is a
modern sanctuary, theatre and chapel, commissioned by Citicorp from Hugh Stubbins and
Associates in 1977 to replace the original church
which was built in 1904. The granite exterior
was designed in a block-like form to distinguish
it from the gleaming aluminium of the surrounding building, and to symbolize the rock, a
reference to Peter, on which Christ would found
his church. Erol Beker designed the Chapel of
the Good Shepherd in which Louise Nevelson
(1899–1988) executed wall sculptures depicting *The Cross of the Good Shepherd, The Trinity,
Sky Vestment, Grapes and Wheat Lintel* and *The
Cross of the Resurrection.*

The Pierpont Morgan Library contains the outstanding collection of books, prints, manuscripts and drawings assembled by J. Pierpont Morgan between 1890 and 1913, and housed in the neo-Renaissance building he commissioned from McKim, Mead & White in 1902.

In 1991 an ambitious programme of expansion incorporated Morgan's house as an annexe to the library. The house, also of a derivative Renaissance design, but executed in the vernacular 'brownstone' of New York, was begun in 1928 under the direction of Benjamin Wistar. The new arrangement allows visitors to enter through the annexe, where period rooms of Pierpont Morgan's residence can still be seen, through the new glass-covered court to join the main building. McKim's design, influenced by the Nymphaeum of Villa Giulia in Rome, was intended to evoke the monumentality of ancient buildings and stand out in New York for its gleaming white marble. $50,000 was spent on the construction of the masonry alone. McKim wanted to recreate the technique of perfectly locking each block with its neighbour without resorting to mortar.

The wealth and power of Morgan or 'Pontifex Morgan' as he was dubbed, was so great that he is said to have single-handedly rescued the American economy during the crisis of 1895. In his collecting he was advised by his nephew Junius Morgan, and by his formidable cataloguer Belle da Costa Greene. As was the case with the art he bought, most of which was sold at his death, his purchases were typically grandiloquent, and sometimes not of the highest quality. However, the scale of his acquisitions was such that Morgan frequently succeeded in buying the best and most rare.

The holdings of the Library are exhibited on a revolving basis, by means of thematic exhibitions of varying scale. At any one time it might be possible to see the 1455 Gutenberg Bible or the ninth-century Lindau Gospels, or some of the nine thousand drawings.

Address
29 East 36th Street
New York, N.Y. 10016
✆ 212 685 0610

Map reference
㉙

How to get there
Subway: 6.
Bus: M1, M2, M3, M4, M34, and M98.

Opening times
Tue to Fri 10.30–5. Sat 10.30–6. Sun 12–6.
Closed Mon.

Entrance fee
Suggested contribution $5 adults; $3 students and senior citizens.

Tours
Tue and Thur at 2.30 tours of the period rooms.
Wed and Fri at 2.30 tours of the main exhibition.

ROCKEFELLER CENTER

Built 1932–40

Address
Fifth Avenue between 48th
and 51st Streets

Map reference

How to get there
Subway: 1, 9, B, D, E, F,
N, R.
Bus: M1, M2, M3, M4, M5,
M6, M7, M27, M32.

Opening times
Open at all times.

Entrance fee
Free.

A testament to ideal and successful urban planning, the construction of the Rockefeller Center, a six-block complex of nineteen buildings, streets, fountain and vistas was begun in 1929. When John D. Rockefeller Jr. embarked on the project he instructed that it should be 'as beautiful as possible consistent with maximum income.' The use of an Art Deco style served to complement the modern aspirations of this 'city within a city' which embraces so fully the metropolitan features of Manhattan – primarily the street grid and tower block. Despite its central location, the design of the Rockefeller Center has one predominant aspect, from Fifth Avenue looking west down Channel Gardens to the fountain and RCA Building rising above. Indeed the buildings gradually get taller as they back onto Sixth Avenue, and the sense of verticality intended for the RCA building is enhanced by the horizontal approach of Channel Gardens and the relatively low buildings which flank it. A stylistic uniformity in the group of buildings was established by using the same Indiana limestone throughout for all exterior surfaces, and articulating each face with similar vertical planes.

The formal purity and sleek construction typical of the International School makes the Seagram Building appear one of the more effortless of the Manhattan towers. However, the insistence of Mies van der Rohe (1886–1969) on the highest quality of detailing and materials made it among the most expensive of the great skyscrapers. The metal structure that supports the glass curtain-walling is cast from bronze of rich and subtly reflective properties. Van der Rohe was assisted on the project by his follower, Philip Johnson, who said of the influence of the building: '…it gave everyone a licence – I am doing Mies!'

Acclaim for this supreme example of modernist confidence was to some extent enhanced by the restaurant on the first floor designed by Philip Johnson. Not only was this one of the first applications of International style interior decoration to a restaurant, but its fame was also enhanced by the sophisticated art that was bought for it, including canvases by Rothko (although these were never installed), and a Picasso stage backdrop of 1929 for *Le Tricorne*.

Address
375 Park Avenue between 52nd and 53rd Streets
New York

Map reference

How to get there
Subway: 6, E, F.
Bus: M1, M2, M3, M4, M101, M102.

Opening times
During business hours.

Entrance fee
Free.

THE STATUE OF LIBERTY

Created 1875–84

Address
Liberty Island

Map reference

How to get there
Boats from Battery Park
leave daily between 9.30
and 3.30 on the hour, and
on the half hour at peak
season. For Information
ring: Circle Line on 212 269
5755

Opening times
Daily 9.30–5.00.
Closed 25 Dec.

Entrance fee
Admission free. Boat $6.00
adults; $3.00 children aged
3–17 years. $5 senior
citizens.

The Statue of Liberty, or Liberty Enlightening
the World, was intended as a gift to America
from the citizens of France. The statue is based
on traditions of colossal sculpture, such as the
famed figure which towered above the harbour
at Rhodes, and bears Classical symbols including the Phrygian bonnet, its seven points relating to the world's continents. The figure carries
a Masonic tablet with *4th of July, 1776* inscribed
on it. Frédéric-Auguste Bartholdi was the sculptor, and the ambitious engineering behind this
colossus was devised by Gustave Eiffel, who
designed the Parisian tower. The first significance
intended for the monument was conceived by
French republicans attempting to draw attention
to the failings of the Second Empire by lionising
American ideals of democratic freedom. The
statue was made in Bartholdi's studio in Paris,
where a skin of repoussé copper weighing eighty-
eight tons was riveted over Eiffel's sprung iron
skeleton, and for ten years it remained there
while a campaign in America raised funds for the
construction of its base. As well as an icon of
democracy, the figure has been a beacon for
generations of immigrants.

Gertrude Vanderbilt Whitney, the founder of the Whitney Museum of American Art, was rich and well-established. Both sides of her family had enormous fortunes and respected social credentials. She, however, was interested and actively involved in the contemporary arts. A sculptress whose studio was renowned as a meeting place, from 1914 she established a succession of organizations to help artists work and exhibit. The Whitney Studio Club, which she set up in 1918, existed for ten years and was the venue for Edward Hopper's first one man show. When the Studio Club came to an end, the Whitney Studio Galleries took their place until 1930, when Mrs. Whitney offered her collection to the Metropolitan Museum. On their refusal to accept the contemporary art she had been assembling, which included the work of artists such as George Bellows, Stuart Davis and Reginald Marsh, she determined to set up her own museum.

The first location of the museum was at 10 West Eighth Street where the six hundred works donated by Mrs. Whitney were shown in three adapted brownstones. As the collection grew the museum moved to West Fifty-fourth Street in 1954, and finally to the present site on Madison Avenue in 1966. Marcel Breuer, the Bauhaus-trained architect was responsible for the design of the museum, which he described as having the vitality of the streets, the latitude of a bridge, and the weight of a skyscraper. The massive block-like structure of the building, which is faced in grey granite, has led to this style of architecture being dubbed 'Brutalist'. Much of this sense of weight and drama derives from Breuer's treatment of the facade, three cantilevered projections which become gradually shallower as they approach the ground. The extensive holdings of the museum are exhibited on a revolving basis on one floor of the six. The remaining space is allocated for temporary exhibitions amongst which the Whitney Biennial has established an international reputation.

Address
945 Madison Avenue
New York, N.Y. 10021
✆ 212 570 3600

Map reference
③

How to get there
Subway: 6
Bus: M2, M3, M4

Opening times
Wed, Fri, Sat, Sun 11–6.
Thur 1–8.
Closed Mon, Tue.

Entrance fee
$7 adults, $5 students. $3 senior citizens 62 and over, free for children under 12.

Tours
Wed-Sun free gallery tours.

★ Early Sunday Morning

1930

Edward Hopper

Early Sunday Morning is one of 2,000 paintings and drawings, bequeathed to the Whitney by the artist's widow. This example is characteristic of works by Hopper (1882–1967) which tend to be concerned with consistently urban, man-made scenes redolent of human presence but void of much action or incident. Even when there are people shown in his paintings they are usually seen to be isolated, alienated or uncommunicative. The design of *Early Sunday Morning* is insistently rectilinear; the street block fills the width of the canvas and its horizontal and vertical divisions fall perfectly into line with the frame. Although the scene contains scattered evidence of everyday commerce and interaction – the faint lettering on the shop windows, fire hydrant and barber pole – they only serve to make the scene appear more empty. What enlivens the vacant block is the sunlight streaming across the walls, picking out vivid colours and solid forms against the flatness of the buildings. Although the sun is not represented, the long shadows cast by the shop signs indicate quite precisely its position. Furthermore the depiction of the precise moment of the sun's passage over the neighbourhood sparks off a sense of nostalgia in the spectator for the curious contradictions of a lifeless but glorious Sunday morning in the silent town.

WHITNEY MUSEUM

Although he was born in the Ukraine, Alexander Archipenko (1887–1964) lived in Paris from 1908, and then the United States from 1923. In 1928 he became a naturalized American citizen. This piece dates from 1935 during which time he was living in California and teaching at the art school he had set up in Los Angeles. Partly due to his own talent, and partly through the absence of any native developments in sculpture at that stage, Archipenko became a highly influential artist in America. The majority of his sculptures were figurative and executed in a rather complex Cubist idiom, but *Torso in Space*, the subject of a number of sculptures and pictures in several media such as drawings, lithographs and collage reliefs, stands out for its formal refinement and simplicity. This version in the collection of the Whitney Museum was executed in metalized terracotta, a medium which gives the sinuous sculpture a sense of warmth, but also a sheen which complements the understated reliefs and curves of the piece. As a purely formal exercise, all extraneous members such as the head and limbs are missing from this figure. But the result is not one of severance or truncation, rather the harmonious core of the torso suggests an essential and curiously expressive body.

Woman with Bicycle

1950

Willem
de Kooning

Willem de Kooning (born 1904) was one of the central artists in the Abstract Expressionist group or New York School. It was his immediate and inspirational style of painting that led the art critic Harold Rosenberg to coin the term 'Action Painting', although this has latterly become associated with the work of Pollock rather than de Kooning. The artist first embarked on painting a series of works devoted to women in 1950, only to become discouraged with the results soon after. However, he was urged to proceed with the theme by the scholar Meyer Shapiro, and by 1953 he had enough material to constitute an important exhibition. A great part of de Kooning's paintings glory in a rich and sensuous application of paint, regardless of the subject matter, a quality which he also admires in other painters' work: 'I've always been crazy about Soutine... Maybe it's the lushness of the paint... There's a kind of transfiguration, a certain fleshiness, in his work.'

De Kooning's *Women*, with Warhol's iconic divas, Lichtenstein's bimbos, and other pin-ups of Pop Art, trace a rich and often ironic relationship between commercial and fine art in Post-war America. *Woman with Bicycle* owes much of its brash frontality to the crass demonstrativeness of advertising. The displacement of the figure's teeth, which have fallen rock-like from her grinning visage, introduces a further note of discord to what started, in its commercial form, as an image of supreme confidence.

Three Flags is just one of a series of paintings executed by Johns (born 1930) on the theme of the American flag . When they were exhibited in 1958 at the Leo Castelli Gallery they proved highly controversial in that they seemed irreverent at best and at worst almost sacrilegious. The artist's throwaway comment on the series cannot have been other than disingenuous: 'Using the design of the American flag took care of a great deal for me because I didn't have to design it.' Johns's appropriation of the Stars and Stripes is very subtle. None of the paintings can really be said to challenge the iconic authority of the flag; they remain crisply exhibited to the extent that the pictures of the flags fall neatly in line with the dimensions of the canvas: they are never shown creased, furled or other than immaculate. The main alteration Johns imposes is a subtle range of painterly effects through his use of the ancient medium of encaustic. Beyond that, one of the paintings is white, another has the form of faces softly emerging behind it, another is doubled. The painting in the Whitney features three overlapping flags which raises one of the most complex debates in modernism, that of the 'reality' of painting. If the three flags are seen to overlap, that presumes that they are material sheets, capable of solid layers, rather than simply layers of paint.

WOOLWORTH BUILDING

Built 1913

Address
233 Broadway between
Barclay Street and Park
Place, New York
℡ 212 553 32000

Map reference
(34)

How to get there
Subway: A, C, E, R, M, N, Z,
4, 5, 6.
Bus: M1, M6, M15, M9.

Opening times
Open daily 8:30–4.

Entrance fee
Free.

For thirteen years, until 40 Wall Street was completed in 1929, the Woolworth Building was the tallest in the world. It was built by the founder of the five- and ten-cent store, F.W. Woolworth, a man who had started life as a farm worker but by 1913 was able to spend $13,500,000 on his 'Cathedral of Commerce'. Since it was constructed before zoning restrictions were introduced in 1916, the base of the tower covers the whole area of its site. Woolworth wanted a design based on the Gothic Revival he admired in London's Houses of Parliament. Accordingly the exterior of the building is adorned with limestone detailing up to the first three floors, and terracotta tiles from there on up. At the second floor are found four masks signifying Europe, Africa, Asia and America, and at the 26th, 49th and 51st floor are gargoyles in the form of beasts including bats, pelicans and frogs. The building was inaugurated with great ceremony: from Washington, President Wilson, alerted by a telegrapher, pushed a button that lit the 80,000 lights needed to illuminate the whole building.

The author and publishers would like to thank the following individuals, museums, galleries and photographic archives for their kind permission to reproduce the following illustrations:

Collection of The New-York Historical Society: 6, 7
The Permanent Collection of The Museum of American Folk Art: 8a (Gift of the Trustees of the Museum of American Folk Art), 94 (photo Gavin Ashworth), 95 (Promised anonymous gift P2.1984.1).
The Brooklyn Museum: 8b & 23 (Dick S.Ramsay Fund 40.340), 22 (Dick S. Ramsay Fund, Governing Committee of The Brooklyn Museum and Anonymous Donors, 66.5), 24 (Sustaining Membership Fund, A. T. White Memorial Fund, A. Augustus Healy Fund 23.98), 25 (Dick S. Ramsay Fund 58.158)
Copyright The Frick Collection: 9, 43, 44, 45, 46, 47, 48, 49, 50
All rights reserved, The Metropolitan Museum of Art: 10a & 74 (Gift of Mr. & Mrs. Charles Wrightsman 1978 (1978.517)), 10b (Arthur Hoppock Hearn Fund 1916 (16.53)), 13 (The Cloisters, on loan from Spain), 34 (The Cloisters Collection 1956 (56.70)), 35a (The Cloisters Collection, Gift of John D.Rockefeller, Jnr. 1937 (37.80.6)), 35b (The Cloisters Collection 1963 (63.12recto)), 63 (Given to the United States by Egypt in 1965, awarded to The Metropolitan Museum of Art in 1967, and installed in the Sackler Wing in 1978)), 64a (Rogers Fund 1903 (03.14.5)), 64b (Rogers Fund 1913 (13.96.14)), 65a (Bequest of Michael Friedsam 1931. The Friedsam Collection (32.2100.43)), 65b (Rogers Fund 1919 (19.164)), 66 (Anonymous gift 1932 (32.130.2)), 67 (Bequest of Mrs.H.O.Havemeyer 1929. The H.O. Havemeyer Collection (29.100.16)), 68 (Munsey Fund 1936 (36.29)), 69 (Gift of Mr. & Mrs. Charles Wrightsman 1981 (1981.238)), 70 (Bequest of Benjamin Altman 1913(13), 71 (Bequest of Mrs. H.O. Havemeyer 1929. The H.O. Havemeyer Collection 1929 (29.100.6)), 72(Gift of Henry G.Marquand 1889 (89.15.21)), 73(Purchased with special funds & gifts of friends of the museum 1961 (61.198)), 75 (Munsey Fund 1934 (34.138)), 76 (Wentworth Fund 1949(49.24)), 77 (The Jules Bache Collection 1949 (49.7.41)), 78 (Wolfe Fund 1931. Catherine Lorillard Wolfe Collection (31.44)), 79 (Reisinger Fund 1926 (26.90)), 80 (Gift of Harry Payne Bingham 1940 (40.175)), 81 (Bequest of Mrs. H.O.Havemeyer 1929. The H.O.Havemeyer Collection (29.100.115)), 82 (Gift of the artist 1923 (23.101)), 83 (Bequest of Mrs.H.O. Havemeyer 1929. The H.O.Havemeyer Collection(29.100.128)), 84 (Wolfe Fund 1907. Catherine Lorillard Wolfe Collection (07.122)), 85 (Bequest of Stephen C.Clark 1960 (61.101.17)), 86 (Bequest of Stephen C.Clark 1960 (61.101.1)), 87 (Bequest of Sam A.Lewisohn 1951 (51.112.2)), 88 (Gift of John Stewart Kennedy 1897 (97.34)), 89 (Catherine Lorillard Wolfe Collection. Purchase 1927, Wolfe Fund (27.67)), 90 (Purchase. Bequest of Emily Crane Chadbourne 1972 (1972.60.1). Installation through the generosity of Saul P.Steinberg and Reliance Group Holdings, Inc. (1972.60.1)), 91 (Bequest of Gertrude Stein 1946 (47.106) © DACS 1995), 92 (George A.Hearn Fund 1957 (57.92) © ARS, N.Y. and DACS, London 1995)
Angelo Hornak: 11a, 13, 19, 20, 28, 38, 39, 52, 116, 117, 119, 124.
Collection of The Whitney Museum of American Art: 11b (Oil on canvas 76.2 x 63.5 cm. Purchase 53.46), 12b (Watercolour on paper 36.5 x 54.9 cm. Purchase 32.42), 120 (Oil on canvas 88.9 x 152.4 cm. Purchase, with funds from Gertrude Vanderbilt Whitney 31.426), 121 (Terracotta, metalized with bronze on painted wood base 76.2 x 147.3 x 41 cm. Gift of Mr. & Mrs. Peter Rubel 58.24a-b), 122 (Oil on canvas 194.3 x 124.5 cm.

Purchase 55.35 © ARS,N.Y. and DACS, London 1995), 123 (Encaustic on canvas 78.4 x 115.6 x 12.7 cm. 50th Anniversary Gift of the Gilman Foundation, Inc., The Lauder Foundation, A. Alfred Taubman, an anonymous donor, and purchase 80.32. © Jasper Johns/DACS, London/VAGA, New York 1995)
The Museum of Modern Art: 12a (Oil on canvas 181 x 219.1 cm. Mrs. Simon Guggenheim Fund. © Succession H. Matisse/DACS 1995), 14a (Oil on canvas 223.4 x 194.4 cm Sidney & Harriet Janis Collection Fund. © ARS,N.Y. and DACS, London 1995), 14b(Oil silkscreened on canvas 91.7 x 61 cm. Elizabeth Bliss Parkinson Fund. © The Warhol Foundation, 1965), 98 (Oil on canvas 73.6 x 93.2 cm. Gift of Mrs. David M. Levy), 99 (Oil on canvas 243.9 x 233.7 cm. Acquired through the Lillie P.Bliss Bequest. © DACS 1995), 100 (Oil on canvas 199.3 x 301 cm. Mrs. Simon Guggenheim Fund), 101(Oil on canvas 127 x 127 cm. Given anonymously), 102 (Bronze 137 x 2 x 21.6 x 16.5 cm. Given anonymously. © ADAGP, Paris and DACS, London 1995), 103(Oil on canvas 129.5 x 200.7 cm. Gift of Mrs.Simon Guggenheim), 104 (Oil on canvas 269.7 x 390.1 cm. Gift of Nelson A.Rockefeller in honor of Alfred H. Barr, Jnr. © Succession H. Matisse /DACS 1995), 105 (Fur-covered cup,saucer & spoon, overall height 7.3 cm, saucer diameter 23.7 cm. Purchase. © DACS 1995), 106 (Oil on canvas 73.7 x 92.1 cm. Purchase. © ADAGP, Paris and DACS, London 1995), 107 (Oil on canvas 24.1 x 33 cm.Given anonymously. © DEMART PRO ARTE BV/DACS 1995), 108a (Collage of shingles, needlepoint, page from the Concordance, pressed flowers, and ferns 50.8 x 54 cm. Gift of Philip L.Goodwin (by exchange)), 108b (Oil on canvas 101.6 x 132.1 cm. Gift of Mrs.Gertrude A. Mellon. © Estate of Stuart Davis/DACS, London/VAGA, New York 1995), 109 (Tempera on gessoed panel 81.9 x 121.3 cm. Purchase. © Andrew Wyeth, 1995), 110 (Oil on canvas 192.1 x 151.4 cm. Mrs.Simon Guggenheim Fund. © ADAGP, Paris and DACS, London 1995), 111 (Oil on canvas 126.7 x 157.5 cm. Gift of Mr. & Mrs.William A.M.Burden. © ADAGP, Paris and DACS, London 1995), 112 (Oil on linen 198.7 x 137.8 cm. William A.M.Burden Fund), 113a (Synthetic polymer paint, silkscreened, & oil on canvas 211.4 x 144.7 cm. Gift of Philip Johnson. © The Warhol Foundation, 1962), 113b (Painted steel 244.5 x 252.7 x 216.5 cm. Mrs Simon Guggenheim Fund (by exchange) and gift of Candida and Rebecca Smith. © Estate of David Smith/DACS London/VAGA, New York 1995)
The New York Public Library: 15 (Astor, Lenox and Tilden Foundations)
Dia Center for the Arts: 16 (photo Bill Jacobson)
Nicholas Ross: 18, 21, 26, 27, 29, 30, 31, 32, 36, 37, 40, 42, 51, 60, 62, 93, 96, 97, 114, 115, 118
The Forbes Magazine Collection: 41
Solomon R. Guggenheim Museum: 53 & 54 (Photo David Heald © The Solomon R. Guggenheim Foundation, New York), 55 (Photo Robert E.Mates © The Solomon R. Guggenheim Foundation, New York 45.961. © ADAGP, Paris and DACS, London 1995), 56a(Gift, Katherine S.Dreier Estate 1953. Photo Robert E.Mates © The Solomon R.Guggenheim Foundation, New York 53.1348. © DACS 1995), 56b (© 1988, The Estate of Robert Mapplethorpe)
Courtesy of The Hispanic Society of America: 57, 58, 59
The Jewish Museum: 61a, 61b (© George Segal/DACS, London/VAGA, New York 1995)

The author would also like to thank Milton Gendel, Monica Incisa, Anita Alessandri, Sarah Carr Gomm, Romana McEwen, Ged Birch, Charlie Mathias, Caroline and Mark Owen-Lloyd, Tony Jenkins, Tor Seidler, Tim Husband, Ashton Hawkins, Caroline Bugler, Julia Brown, Nick Ross, Keith Glutting, John Doyle, Cristina Alfonso, Daniel Kletke, and Michele Marincola.

INDEX

Index of Artists, Sculptors, Architects and Photographers
Figures in bold refer to main entries

INDEX

A note on the itineraries

The following itineraries are designed for those with a week to spend in New York. They have been arranged as far as possible in order of importance, although the suggested combinations for each day have also been dictated by practical concerns such as location and ease of travel from one attraction to another. It should be possible to view all the items suggested on each day's itinerary, but visitors may well chose to proceed at a more leisurely rate and select one or two locations from each morning or afternoon according to their individual tastes rather than attempt to see everything listed. Those with limited time should focus on the starred items. The numbers in circles beside each location are map references. Works of art within the galleries and museums are arranged in the order that they are most likely to be seen by the visitor.

The entry fees and times of opening are correct at the time of publication, but they may be liable to change without notice.

DAY 1 MORNING

✪ **METROPOLITAN MUSEUM OF ART** ㉓
(p.62)
Closed Mondays

Temple of Dendur (p.63)
Frescoes from Boscoreale (p.64)
**Head of a Bodhisattva, perhaps
Siddhartha** (p.64)
Francesco d'Este
Rogier van der Weyden (p.65)
✪ **The Harvesters** (p.65)
Pieter Bruegel the Elder
The Adoration of the Magi
Andrea Mantegna (p.66)
Portrait of a Young Man
Agnolo Bronzino (p.67)
Venus and the Lute Player
Titian (p.68)
**Rubens, his wife, Helena
Fourment, and their son Peter Paul**
Sir Peter Paul Rubens (p.69)
Portrait of Lucas van Uffele
Sir Anthony van Dyck (p.70)
✪ **View of Toledo**
El Greco (p.71)
Lady with a Water Jug
Jan Vermeer (p.72)
✪ **Aristotle with a Bust of Homer**
Rembrandt van Rijn (p.73)
Penitent Magdalene
Georges de la Tour (p.74)
Mezzetin
Jean-Antoine Watteau (p.75)
Boy Blowing Bubbles
Jean-Baptiste-Siméon Chardin (p.76)
Don Manuel Ossorio de Zuñiga
Francisco de Goya (p.77)
The Death of Socrates
Jacques-Louis David (p.78)

DAY 1 AFTERNOON

✪ **METROPOLITAN MUSEUM OF ART** ㉓
(p.62)
Closed Mondays

The Island of the Dead
Arnold Böcklin (p.79)
Young Ladies of the Village
Gustave Courbet (p.80)
Boating
Edouard Manet (p.81)
Lady at a Tea Table
Mary Cassatt (p.82)
Woman with Chrysanthemums
Edgar Degas (p.83)
**Madame Charpentier and her
Children**
Pierre-Auguste Renoir (p.84)
✪ **La Parade**
Georges Seurat (p.85)
Card Players
Paul Cézanne (p.86)
✪ **Ia Orana Maria**
Paul Gauguin (p.87)
Washington Crossing the Delaware
Emanuel Leutze (p.88)
The Wyndham Sisters
John Singer Sargent (p.89)
**Room from the Francis W. Little
House**
Frank Lloyd Wright (p.90)
Portrait of Gertrude Stein
Pablo Picasso (p.91)
Autumn Rhythm (Number 30)
Jackson Pollock (p.92)

CLEOPATRA'S NEEDLE ⑩ (p.31)